FLORIDA
ROOTS
NAVY
WINGS

Thanks to Rae Smith, a fine
Georgia Tech engineer that is
now engineering on people
We shall not like this people

Sam Davis
7/5/04

To "Walter"!
Let's not let decades
pass again —
Lona Spencer

FLORIDA ROOTS NAVY WINGS

by
Lt. Cdr. Samuel A. Davis, USNR (Ret.)

as told to
Lona Davis Spencer

Phone (813) 234-8432
LLeafPress@aol.com
(Please Print):

Name _____

Address _____

City_____

State _____Zip _____

e-mail _____

Send your order with payment to:
Longleaf Press, Inc.
5008 N. 9th St.
Tampa, FL 33603-2302
ISBN 0-9652270-0-6

FLORIDA ROOTS, NAVY WINGS

Copyright © 1996 by Samuel A. Davis
and Lona Davis Spencer

ISBN 0-9652270-0-6

Book design by Melissa Bowden
Trey Andrews, cover illustration

Manufactured in the United States of America

Longleaf Press
P.O. Box 9837
Tampa, Florida 33674-9837

To Mary Lona Forgy Davis
and
Thomas M. Spencer,
without whom
this book could not have been written.

To Jonathan E. Spencer,
for whom this book is written.

WINGS
AND WATERS

M y grandson's godmother gave him a plaque that says "There are only two lasting bequests we can give our children — one is roots, the other, wings." My folks gave me both. Our roots were firmly planted in the sandy soil of West Florida. I lived in a Florida linked by its waterways, in communities knit together by shared rides on the mailboats. I never lived more than 50 miles from a bay, gulf, sea, or ocean. My wings were forged by an educated Mama and an ambitious Daddy. They wanted to better themselves, and they wanted a better life for their children — simple notions but profound in their effect. My life was shaped by the wings I have known: the soaring hopes of my parents; the golden wings of the U.S. Navy; the wings of the airplanes I flew; and the guardian angel wings that time and again have shielded me and mine from danger. When I was a young man, I had the unutterable privilege to fly the best wings over the greatest waters of the earth. This is my story.

BORN ON THE
FLORIDA FRONTIER

My Daddy was tough as a boiled owl, and my Mama was the schoolmaster's daughter. They lived on a frontier that bears no resemblance to the tame bug-sprayed Florida of Yankee dreams. He was from a line of boatmen, able to put anything on water anywhere he wanted it. She had snapping brown eyes and was a genius with people. He was Pasco. She was Nell. I am their youngest child, Sam.

My people were wanderers. The Davises came from Wales to the American continent, first to Georgia, then Alabama, Tennessee, and Mississippi, finally reaching Calhoun County, Florida. My grandfather, Lewis Cass Davis, fought at the battle of Marianna, Florida, in the Confederate Army to keep Union troops out of Tallahassee. He married Josephine Stone and moved his family out of the malaria infested inland to the more healthful Gulf of Mexico coast at Allanton, Florida.

The gulf breezes kept the mosquitos down, at least compared to the calmer air of Calhoun County. My Grandma and Grandpa Davis settled in an area that wasn't yet Bay County when my Daddy was born there. My Grandmother Davis's family was English. The Stones went to Virginia first. One of the family, Thomas Stone, came to Savannah, Georgia, and became a member of the Georgia legislature. Its sessions were held at his establishment, the "Coffee House." While meeting there on January 28, 1785, the House Assembly of Georgia granted a charter to the Board of Trustees of the University of Georgia, the first charter issued in the United States to a state university.

A number of Stones went further south to Calhoun County where they acquired considerable land on the west side of the Apalachicola

River, in a river port called Iola near the town of Wewahitchka. The Stones intermarried with the Yon family from Virginia, some of whom had filtered into Florida. I had a great many uncles Stone and Yon. We were the Samuel Pasco Davis family.

I was born on my Daddy's homestead in Farmdale at the head of East St. Andrew's Bay, 20 miles from the county seat Panama City. The old ship's pass from the Gulf of Mexico came into St. Andrew's Bay around Red Fish Point. Panama City is on the north side of the Bay opposite the new ship's pass, dredged out in 1935. From there the Bay fans out in three directions, forming North, West, and East St. Andrew's Bays. Farmdale was on the east side, as the 18th and 19th century settlers weren't interested in the salt soil and worse, hurricane damage, in what became Panama City Beach to the west.

Farmdale linked family settlements all along East Bay and its feeder creeks and bayous. In Farmdale itself we had a grammar school, a post office, and a dock for the mailboat. We even had a hotel until it burned down. Al Fay, our nearest neighbor, said it was 25 miles to town one way and 75 miles the other. When asked for an explanation, he replied, "It's 25 miles with the wind and 75 miles against." That wasn't just country-boy humor — we had to tack a sailboat back and forth when traveling against the wind. Al Fay lived a half-mile away from us. Grammar school was 2 1/2 miles from my home — a half mile by foot, one and a half miles by boat (with the wind), a last half mile by foot on into Farmdale proper.

We Davis children took this daily trip with our nearest neighbors — Laurene, Joyce, Iva Jean, Roy David, and Steve Daniels. Some days on the way to school we fussed with each other, and other days we caught tadpoles in the ditchwater together. Their father, Frank Daniels, was the stiller at my Uncle Mood's turpentine still.

When I was six years old and my brother Carl was eight, I fell into the water on my way home from school. Carl started screaming. Frank Daniels ran out of the still and realized I was not beside my brother in the boat — Carl and I were so inseparable that where you found one of us you found the other. Carl had the presence of mind to point to where I'd sunk into the water beside the dock. Frank jumped in and pulled me out. Even though I couldn't swim and Carl was petrified with fear, my life was saved because Frank

Daniels was quick to my rescue. I never forgot how deadly water can be when you're careless, and I never lost my gratitude to my rescuer.

All of us in Farmdale traveled by foot, horse or boat. We got to the ice cream and electricity in town three or four times a year on the mailboat, a 40 foot motor launch with a passenger's cabin. The mailboat started its run at Overstreet on Wetappo Creek in the early morning, about 4 a.m. They picked up mail at Wetappo, at Allanton, then ran across the bay to Farmdale. From our community they went to Belle Isle, then to Auburn, before crossing back over the East Bay to Cook and on to Callaway. They recrossed the bay south to San Blas and Cromanton, before crossing north again to Parker, Bay Harbor, and Millville, in that order. They finally arrived in Panama City at noon.

When the train from Dothan, Alabama, came and went out again, the mail boat started the same run in reverse order, arriving back at Overstreet usually by 9 p.m. It carried a limited amount of freight and passengers. The mailboat brought Dr. D. M. Adams, Sr., out to our place for my birth on June 7, 1917. My sister Eloise remembers being hustled out to a neighbor's house that she loved to visit. This kindly neighbor told her that when she went home there would be a big surprise waiting for her.

Eloise dearly wanted a doll she had seen in town; she knew that the family had been unable to afford to buy it for her. As time went by, she became certain that the doll would be at the house when she went back home. She joined in what was clearly excited anticipation in the adults around her. Finally, the neighbor led Eloise back home. Daddy took her into the house to see her big surprise. It was me, not the beautiful doll. I was a major disappointment. Eloise suggested that since she already had two brothers, Jim and Carl, could we exchange me for the doll anyway?

My parents were expecting a girl, and they had no boy's names for me. They decided quickly that I was probably the last child, so "Samuel" after my Daddy would do. They had no middle name, however. Doc Adams was at the house for hours, waiting for me to emerge at 3:15 p.m., then for the mailboat to take him back to town. He would record my birth at the county courthouse, but I had to have a name. For some reason my normally sensible Mama couldn't find a middle name she liked. Daddy wouldn't stand for "Junior." Finally, Doc Adams went out into the yard. He said, "Pasco, I have to catch the boat. I can't spend any more time out here. I'll name this baby myself if y'all don't."

My father said, "Well, Doc, you name him."

"Alright, Pasco, I'll name him after me. He's Samuel Adams Davis."

This solution pleased both of my parents. I was named by and for their old friend Doc.

From my earliest life I remember the way Mama handled us children when we ran to her with tales of injustice. I'd say something like, "Mama, Steve Daniels hit me!"

She would say, "What did you do?"

"I hit him back!"

"And before he hit you?"

"Well, I sort of kicked him. But he hit me!"

"And what did you do?"

"I didn't mean to kick him, not really."

"If you were kicked, what would you do?"

With a series of patient questions, Mama gleaned the real story and showed us how one thing led to another. By that time, we weren't getting anywhere in the righteous wrath department. Eventually each of us learned not to try to tattle to Mama.

I suppose opposites really do attract and marry each other sometimes. There was a fierce edge to my Daddy and his brothers. My Uncle George epitomized the philosophy "Root hog or die poor." He died as Captain Davis with the Dixie Fleet deep-sea fishing boats, not poor. My Uncle John built his home on the Intracoastal Waterway from concrete blocks he made himself on the property. My cousins still live on the land he secured on East St. Andrew's Bay. My Uncle Mood had a Pier and Recreation Hall that lasted until the government took his land for Tyndall Field. All our farming community courted there, and I still sneak over there to fish in the shallow waters among the submerged pilings, all that's left. Daddy wrested a military pension for Mama's father from three levels of government, especially notable since Grandpa Russell served in the Confederate Armed Services.

Grandpa Russell was born James Russell Hallam, Jr. As a young man in Kentucky, he and a friend saddled up their horses and rode over to Lexington to enlist themselves and their horses in the Confederate Army. They served in Company K of the 2nd Mounted Infantry, the unit known as Morgan's Raiders. When they lost the Civil War, Grandpa left Kentucky for Alabama where he dropped his surname and styled himself "James Russell." He was a well educated man for his day, so when he moved to Freeport, Florida, he became the schoolmaster. There he married Sara Ellen Evans, and they had three girls and a boy of their own. One of those girls was my mother, Eleanor, called "Nell" for as far back as I can remember. She became a teacher and went to work teaching in Farmdale. Married women were not allowed to teach in those days, so she had to quit when she married my Daddy. She enjoyed her own home more than the scrutiny of various taxpaying families in whose homes she had been required to board as a school teacher.

Daddy told me never to underestimate the power of an educated woman. He often said the best thing he ever did was to marry a smart woman, and Mama was certainly that. She never changed her name to "Hallam," though she joined the Daughters of the American Revolution on the strength of her genealogical research. I think she also joined the DAR to prove she could to the old cat in town who thought Mama's country origins weren't good enough for the Bay County chapter in Panama City. The more sophisticated Hallams welcomed Mama for the long-lost cousin she was.

Mama said that the happiest times of her long life were when the entire family — she and Daddy, my sister, two brothers and me — went in the ox-cart to the Gulf beach east of Farmdale at the head of Crooked Island Sound. We camped on the beach overnight, sometimes spending two nights there. We caught mullet in the cast nets Daddy made and cooked the fish in iron skillets over a fire. We bedded down to the sounds of the Gulf of Mexico surf. We were all within Mama's reach under an open sky.

WANTING MORE

Daddy was a crew member on Cullen Raffield's boat during fishing season. They fished with nets for mullet, mackerel, blue fish, and pompano. Once they put into Port St. Joe to get out of rough weather and moored their boat near a sailing schooner that was loaded with lumber and turpentine still equipment. Daddy saw his Uncle Higdon Stone on the deck of the schooner and called up to him from the fishing boat.

Uncle Hig was in business with George Hardy, a young man from North Carolina. They needed a launch to off-load the schooner and haul the lumber and equipment up onto the shore along the Gulf beyond Six Mile Point. Daddy got Cullen to agree to help them. George Hardy and Uncle Hig hauled the supplies from the beach over the pine woods and set up their turpentine business partnership.

George Hardy supplied the lumber and still, and Uncle Hig owned a sizable acreage of pine woods for their use. Their partnership lasted for many years, and George married Uncle Hig's niece, Annie Stone. They proceeded to have a bunch of what we called "young'uns" — Alton, Max, Willie, Roland, Gertrude, Irene, Adelaide, Quincy, and Raymond.

Every town with a post office seemed to have a turpentine still in those days. Each still had its own dock, barge, and tug boat to haul their turpentine and rosin to Panama City. There the 150 foot steamer Tarpon took these products to either Pensacola or Mobile, then hauled supplies back to the commissary of the company that owned the turpentine still. Each still had its own commissary and houses for its workers and their families. Some of the turpentine companies owned large acreages of timber, while some leased turpentining rights from land owners.

Daddy tapped slash and long-leaf pine trees for their gum, his own trees and trees he leased on others' land. There were six other species of pine in Florida, but they didn't run enough sap to warrant working them. When we children were old enough to reach the cuts on the tree trunks, we worked alongside him.

Daddy first selected a tree and put up the cup, hanging a one quart cup at the base of it. Then with a hack he cut a fish bone slash into the wood, a chevron shape on one face of the trunk. He might put up more than one cup on a tree, but he took care never to girdle his trees with them. The gum ran down the face cut into the cup.

When Daddy began turpentining he had no cups and no money to buy them. Then he cut a cavity into the base of the tree so that the gum ran into it to be dipped out. We called this a box, and all our descriptions of turpentining were about boxes rather than cups.

In about two weeks the cut began to heal up and the gum flow almost ceased. Then Daddy cut another fish bone slash on the same face, about 1/4 inch thick, to expose new resin ducts. This was called "chipping boxes," and he did it every two weeks to each tree.

The cups filled in four to six weeks. When the face cuts got shoulder high, he cut them with a puller, a type of hack mounted on a pole. Pullers and hacks were curved metal pieces with sharpened edges that chipped the bark and a thin shaving of wood away to expose fresh resin ducts. This was called "pulling the boxes," even when cups were used. A crop was 10,000 boxes, about what one man could chip or pull in two weeks.

Dipping crews came in with 5 gallon buckets and dipped the gum from the cup to the bucket. They emptied the buckets into 50 gallon barrels that were loaded on wagons pulled by horses, mules, or oxen.

When all the barrels on a wagon were full, we hauled them to the turpentine still. There we loaded up six barrels of gum into the copper still tank, capped the tank, and attached the cap pipe to a copper tubing worm immersed in a water tank to cool and condense the spirits of turpentine.

We cooked the gum over a wood burning furnace for three hours. The turpentine spirits and water vapor separated after condensing. We put the turpentine in leak-proof barrels. Then we poured the rosin residue from the tanks through wire and cotton batting into a vat. While the rosin was still hot, we dipped it from the vat into barrels to cool for shipping. Sometimes the rosin was so hot that it flamed up when we opened the tank. With turpentine stills throughout the woods, we had a lot of wildfire.

You haven't been hot until you've collected pine sap, distilled turpentine, and cooked rosin in a Florida summer.

In late fall, gum congealed on the face of the trees. By late winter it was thick enough for us to scrape the boxes, use a metal scrape to remove the gum, distill it, and barrel it up.

A distillation of 300 gallons of pine tree gum yielded 100 gallons of spirits of turpentine and 156 gallons of rosin. This was called naval stores operation because cooked gum had been used for centuries to seal cracks in the planks of wooden ships and keep them from leaking. Rosin was used in making paint and varnish, and spirits of turpentine were used for paint thinner, for naval stores, and for civilian purposes. In addition, spirits of turpentine were used in some medicines. The finest rosin went to violinists and fiddlers such as I heard on winter nights on the WSM radio station out of Nashville, Tennessee.

Turpentining was hot, hard, monotonous work that we did to survive. I wanted more out of my life than this.

10-year-old Sam with flounder at Farmdale.

Pasco and Nellie Davis, Sam's parents.

Ready for work;
L to R: Lacey Raffield, Alvin Williams, Luke Cotton, Clayton Raffield,
Cullen Raffield, Henry Cushing

Davis men at Cullen Raffield's boat;
L to R: Al Fay, Mood Davis, John Davis, Pasco Davis, Bart Fay

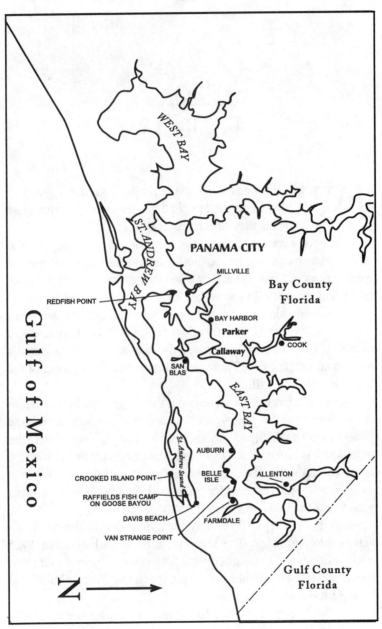

Our part of the world

EARLY
FORESTRY

When I was a child, the turpentine companies generally worked out the trees for turpentine over five to ten years before they cut the trees for timber.

The trees were cut down by two men using a cross-cut saw. The haulers drove mules, or oxen, pulling log carts to drag the logs down to a creek, a river, or a bay. There they rolled the logs into the water and the rafters took over. My Daddy worked for good wages as a rafter.

Daddy and his crew floated the logs around and chained them together to form rafts, usually about 600 to 800 feet long and 150 to 200 feet wide. A tug boat towed the rafts down to the sawmills located around the Bay. There the rafters pulled the logs out of the water up into the mill.

When the large trees were gone, the companies hired men to cut smaller trees for pulpwood. It was incredibly hard work, and almost as hot as distilling turpentine. The heat and humidity in the woods sapped strong men's strength, the insects drove them crazy, and five kinds of poisonous snakes lurked at their feet. When it came time to thin his trees for pulpwood, Daddy often hired other men to cut the trees he selected for them.

By cutting in a profligate way, the lumber companies ran themselves into shortages. The Depression came to Florida in 1925 with a collapse of non-agricultural land values. By then there was too little commercial value left in our forests, and agricultural land values plummeted as well.

As the Depression came to the rest of the nation, large landowners in Florida saw that a "cut out, get out" policy was devastating everybody. Pay plummeted as wealth disappeared in lower and lower market values. Many people had no jobs at all. Drifters came by our farm, hungry men with no family around and no place to live. For weeks at a time they'd work for food and live in our bunkhouse. In some places in town, men stood in line for bread.

As always, my Daddy didn't sit still and let events wash over him. He believed we had to conserve what resources we had left if things were ever going to get better. He talked to as many legislators as would listen to help establish the Florida Forest Service in the 1920s. Daddy and his friends worked on the legislators to start the Forestry School at the University of Florida with faculty trained by the famous forester Gifford Pinchot at Biltmore, George Vanderbilt's chateau in Asheville, North Carolina.

My Daddy and Mama borrowed dibbles from the District Forester N.R. "Zeke" Harding. They dug seedlings from young thicket areas to plant on bare or poorly stocked land. Where his trees naturally reseeded the land, Daddy transplanted them or thinned them out for pulpwood. He fought wildfire to keep it from burning him out every year. When his trees were big enough, Daddy put cattle out among them to graze. Every time he got a little money put by, he bought more forest land or more cows.

We planted close to a thousand acres by hand over the years. My Daddy was so proud of his forests that he readily sold off the waterfront properties he acquired from time to time. He seemed to love those trees, this man I thought was unsentimental, and I learned to care for them, too.

THE GREAT DEPRESSION

In my youth and through high school, jobs were scarce. There was plenty of work our businesses and farms needed done, but no one had any money to pay so a lot of it went undone. Under President Herbert Hoover, the federal government acted on the idea that low government spending would restore large investors' confidence and start economic recovery. But it turned out to be the lack of money altogether that was keeping workers from being hired and stores from selling their wares. There were few taxes being collected because there was nothing produced and nothing sold.

Bay County couldn't pay Mama and the other school teachers anything but scrip, good only at some grocery stores. The DuPont company had acquired about half the timberland acreage in the county. Almost no one else had enough money to pay property taxes. Each year, the county redeemed the scrip from the teachers for real money when DuPont paid their property taxes.

My family got by doing everything we could. We grew vegetables on about ten acres, had beef cattle on the open range, did turpentining on leased land, and did labor odd jobs for a livelihood. I even made 30 cents an hour as a plumber's helper. We took mullet, mackerel, trout, scallops, and oysters from the bay to our table. We ate bacon, sausage, and ham from our own pigs. We ate beef and goat meat from our own herds. We shot ducks and squirrels. Mama regularly shot rabbits who fed on the cabbages, mustard greens, squash, peas, beans, turnips, carrots, and beets in her garden. Just like city people expect, we ate possum occasionally, but it was too greasy to enjoy. I can't remember going hungry. Some years we were reduced to eating only mullet and sweet potatoes, but we never had to go on relief.

But hope for a less arduous life was as scarce as jobs. In 1926, my parents boarded my oldest brother Jim in Panama City for high school. They raked and scraped together everything they could to send him the next year, but they couldn't raise enough money. Jim got a job instead.

In 1928, the county began sending a school bus out to Farmdale. Eloise and Carl went to high school without the expense of boarding in town anymore. They both graduated, and she was valedictorian of her senior class, but Jim never got to go back to school. Being a teacher herself, Mama felt bad all her life that she and Daddy hadn't been able to pay for Jim to stay in Panama City and finish school.

Florida's economy around us began to get better when Franklin D. Roosevelt became President. He told us we had nothing to fear but fear itself, and we believed him.

With government priming the pump, more people could pay the kind of taxes that paved Highway 98. Eloise and Carl had gone to school on the bus over dirt roads, crossing the bay on Melvin Lewis's ferry at Belle Isle. By 1932, I went to Bay High School in Panama City on a fully paved Highway 98.

Government programs put money in people's pockets to buy things. Owners then had the chance to manufacture and supply those things people wanted to buy. I saw factories around us built and put back into production, employing people who made real money for the first time in their lives.

With the New Deal came favorable tax laws for tree-farming. DuPont contracted with the Florida Forest Service to put their land under forest management for protection from wildfire. The company paid three cents an acre for this service, money that had no little part in the success of conservation at the state level. I went to work as a helper on Alton Hardy's Florida Forest Service truck. George Hardy's son had grown up to be a Forest Ranger. We put out wildfires with our water tank trucks and a fire line plow. Later on, Rangers were equipped with a crawler tractor and a fire line plow mounted on a transport that took it close to the fire where they unloaded it and plowed the fire out. But when I was a Ranger's helper, we used our plows to maintain fire lines through the woods in order to help stop wildfire from spreading throughout the area. We didn't think our life was a bad deal. We had a Fourth of July picnic in Farmdale, a Christmas tree at the schoolhouse, Thanksgiving at Grandma Davis's, and occasionally a medicine show came by. But I still wanted more. I wanted ... adventure.

WAR CLOUDS AND THE CIVILIAN

Far away from my home, the greatest "adventure" of the twentieth century was headed my way. On September 18, 1931, Japan invaded Manchuria in northern China. We heard about burning towns and weeping orphans over there. In 1933, Hitler became Chancellor of Germany, and in 1934 he added the office of President of Germany to his titles and styled himself "Fuhrer." Millions of Germans flocked into the Nazi Party. We heard about massive Nazi German rallies. In 1935, Hitler reintroduced the German military draft, won agreement from the British Admiralty to rebuild the German Navy with surface ships and submarines, and announced the creation of an air force — 2000 combat planes in the Luftwaffe.

We heard about all the jobs on long German factory production lines. My forestry job played out as the grass and bushes began to green up in the spring and the summer rains came. Being out of work again, I went to the old Spanish Fort Barrancas at Pensacola for Citizen's Military Training Camp (CMTC) in the summers of 1935 and 1936. I was a private my first summer, a corporal, and then a sergeant my second summer. J. Emory "Red"

Cross was my company commander and a good one. Under the supervision of active duty Army officers and enlisted men, we mastered Army drilling and parade procedures. They taught us how to work 155 millimeter coast artillery guns as a crew. I learned to spot a target towed by a ship, get the range, set the sights, load the gun, fire the missiles, reload, and fire again. A young man could finish all four years of military training at CMTC, with much study and pizzazz, and become an Army officer paid $135 a month as a "Shave Tail" rather than the $21 a month paid to buck privates. I was spurred by a lack of necessary funds. I didn't want to be a soldier for $21 a month.

On July 7, 1937, Japan invaded the rest of China. On March 12, 1938, Hitler annexed Austria. No one moved effectively to stop them. I saw the British Prime Minister Neville Chamberlain on the newsreels, saying he had achieved "peace in our time" by joining France and Italy in signing a peace declaration with Germany on September 30, 1938.

On October 1, Germany took Sudentenland without firing a shot. I didn't know how far Hitler and Emperor Hirohito of Japan would go, but I figured they were bullies, so they wouldn't stop on their own. A bully picks on a little guy, someone who seems like he can't or won't fight back. Eventually the bully takes on a guy too big to beat up. Then that's the end of it. Even in the backwoods of Florida, we knew war was coming to us.

EARLY CONSERVATION

One of the best things President Roosevelt ever created was the Civilian Conservation Corps (the CCC). In our neck of the woods, it provided additional stimulus to landholding companies to begin conservation and put their tree farms back into production. The CCC took unemployed young men and women off the streets to do conservation work in a semi-military camp environment. They learned a trade, ate three meals a day, had a place to live, and earned $25 a month. Dalton Clyde Spann of Slocomb, Alabama, was one of these young men. Clyde grew up on a farm in South Alabama. When he was twelve, his father died unexpectedly, and Clyde became another victim of the sharecropping system in the South. Between the Civil War and World War II, many farmland owners took such profits from their sharecroppers each year that families like Clyde's lived in virtual slavery — never possessing anything of their own, working for the bread that another man ate. Sharecropping was part of a system that kept black and white poor people from getting ahead and bettering themselves. The Southern oligarchy who owned the land benefitted from fostering racial hatred and fear among poor whites and poor blacks. As long as poor people hated and feared each other, they never banded together to change the arrangements, like sharecropping, that kept them poor. Clyde left school after the fifth grade to work ceaselessly, helping his father sharecrop two "one-horse" farms for the bare essentials to support his mother and brothers and sisters. When his father died, Clyde kept both farms going until the CCC was created. When the CCC arrived, he signed right up. He kept $5 a month of his pay for incidental expenses and sent $20 a month home to his mother for food for herself and the younger children. They had not lived this well in years. The CCC taught Clyde forestry from the ground up. He learned on-the-job forest management practices necessary to get sustained yield from trees: selective cutting; natural reseeding of the forest from exemplary seed trees; gathering seed to plant trees; transplanting seedlings to land where no seed trees are available. The CCC conserved the lives of trees and the lives of men. Like all matters of grace and balance, it was a beautiful thing.

THE US BLACKWATER

My Uncle John offered me a job in 1937 as third mess cook on his dredge boat, and I took it. I had learned to cook at nine years of age when Mama went back to teaching school in 1926. Uncle John was captain and Uncle George was chief engineer of the US Blackwater, a Corps of Engineers dredge that was based at the Ingalls Shipyard on the Singing River at Pascagoula, Mississippi. They had originally been hired by Ben Kirkland, who later married their sister, my Aunt Ellen Davis.

The Blackwater was our floating home. We had a walk-in refrigerator and an ice plant. We distilled our own fresh water. We worked three shifts around the clock, so I cooked four meals in a 24-hour day and brewed coffee all day and all night. I made a dark boiled coffee that comforted the rest of the crew on wet, cool nights. It was on the Blackwater that I learned the importance of hot coffee to the American seaman.

Uncle John paid me a salary and room and board. It was my best job yet, and I was on a real ship. We were sailors, although sea-going ships referred to us as muddy water sailors. I didn't care, because dredging was as crucial in our part of the world — for trade, mail, and travel — as any highways or railroads became later. Boats sailing in the channels were our fastest and most reliable transportation.

Channels in the rivers and bays naturally silted up and became too shallow for boats to go through. We dredged this silt up from the bottom of channels with a cutter head dredge and sections of 16" and 24" pipe mounted on pontoons.

We lowered the cutter head to the bottom of the channel ahead of the boat on a boom that extended off the bow. The cutter head rotated in the silt down there. A suction mouth just back of the cutter head sucked the churned-up silt out of the water through the pipes. We pumped the wet silt off the stern of the boat in a pipeline that ran out over pontoons onto a nearby shore. In large bays, we put the end of the pipeline a good distance to the side and away from the channel. In some places we built up spoil islands with the silt we took out of the channels.

I joined the US Blackwater at Bay St. Louis, Mississippi, where we dredged off sandbars in the ship channel. Her run that summer took her next to Destin, Florida, to dredge off sandbars from the Gulf of Mexico into Choctawhatchee Bay. From there she took the Intracoastal Waterway to Overstreet, Florida, and on into the Apalachicola River, keeping channels open where needed. Finally, her run ended upriver at Fort Benning, Georgia. Then she turned around, came back to Mississippi, and began new dredging assignments.

Our speed on the Blackwater was 5 to 7 knots, nautical miles per hour, if we were unhindered by weather or by hav-ing to move the dredge. When we dredged, we made 500 to 1,000 feet in 24 hours. The difference depended on how much bottom silt had to be moved. We strung anchors out from the bow on each side, reaching long distances ahead. The dredge, cutter head and pipe, was mounted at the bow. On the stern were mounted spuds — large wooden pilings fitted with heavy pointed iron feet. The civil engineer on board took depth soundings and calculated the proper depth to set the cutter head. With the dredge moored in the middle of a channel, the leverman signalled the boat engineer to start the cutter head and the pump. Then the leverman dropped the cutter head to the depth to be dredged and raised the port side spud off the bottom.

The starboard spud was dropped so that it stuck in the bottom of the waterway. The leverman reeled in the starboard bow anchor cable, so that the dredge swung in a 45 degree arc to the starboard by pivoting on the lowered spud. The leverman swung the cutter head back and forth at a speed consistent with the depth to be dredged and the amount of silt spoil to be removed. When the dredge had pivoted as far as it could in the starboard direction, the swing was stopped. Then the port spud was lowered and the starboard spud was raised. The leverman reeled in the port bow anchor cable so that the dredge swung back again in a 45 degree arc to the port side. This procedure was continually repeated. On each swing, the dredge boat advanced about 10 feet, as if it walked using the spuds as its feet.

Of course, the dredge stopped for all kinds of things — rock ledges, deep water, snags in the anchor cables, raising and lowering spuds, mechanical breakdowns. But we didn't stop for time clocks or union rules or darkness. When we dredged out a channel, the boat continually inched ahead, pumping and sucking and depositing spoil.

The first day I was on board, we left Bay St. Louis, cruising the Intracoastal Waterway through Mississippi Sound and Canal, into Mobile Bay in Alabama. From Mobile Bay we sailed the Intracoastal Waterway the next day by the Old Spanish Fort Barrancas and the Pensacola Naval Air station. I was on the Blackwater, sailing up the Intracoastal Waterway past the swimming beach at Fort Barrancas when I was hailed by my old CMTC company commander Red Cross.

He called across the water, "Sam! Why aren't you here?"

I yelled back, "This is a regular job, and they're paying me $60.00 a month." That was the hard truth.

In the early 1930s Daddy had rented an excursion boat to take us from Farmdale to Panama City to see the seaplanes docked off the end of Harrison Avenue, U.S. Highway 231. Eloise and I had splashed in the bay underneath one of their big wings. The summer of 1937 as a sailor, I looked across a glassy, smooth Pensacola bay to see the seaplanes of the 1930s, taking off and landing.

Like pelicans, these flying boats seemed to lose their ungainly land characteristics when they took to the air. They flew down onto the water like the largest of seabirds, skimming the water, coming in with plumes of spray like the most elegant rooster tails I had ever seen. When they finally stopped, they sat on the water as improbably as they had hit it, unbroken and intact. Then they did the unimaginable, breaking the bonds of the baywater in long runs that ended with the lift of their wings back into the air where they belonged.

The contrast with the slow work on the dredge boat could not have been greater. I still had a job to do on the Blackwater, but I never forgot those flying boats.

By the time we left Pensacola Bay, the vision of seaplanes was burned into my mind and onto my heart. We sailed into the narrows at Choctawhatchee and through its pass into the Gulf of Mexico at Destin. We dredged the channel there to keep it open to a smaller bay used by small boats. Then we put out to sea in the Gulf of Mexico to go to Panama City. There was no inland waterway linking the two towns then. Because the Blackwater was not a sea-going craft, we always waited for calm weather to make the 70 mile run in the Gulf of Mexico.

That summer when we ran through a school of King mackerel, some of the crew took the motor launch to troll for fish. They caught so many that the other two cooks and I made a fish fry for all hands, enough for two meals. I made Mama's legendary hush puppies.

From Panama City we went right on up through East St. Andrew's Bay to Farmdale. We took the creeks and canal past Overstreet, dredging several miles of shoal water. Late that summer I was on the canal near Overstreet when Alton Hardy drove up in his Florida Forest Service truck. He told me that the Head Ranger was quitting, as he had hired on just to get the St. Joe Forestry Unit started. Alton would be made Unit Ranger, and they wanted me to become Assistant Forest Ranger for the Red Fish to St. Joe area. He asked, "Sam, you want the job? It's yours if you do." I said, "Alton, I'd like to do it, but I can't afford to quit my job here. Last time the Forestry Service didn't pay me this good." "Now Sam, don't you worry. This here pays $60.00 a month. It's being a Ranger, not just a helper. You work all year 'round." That wasn't any more than I was making on the Blackwater, but being a mess cook was seasonal work. An Assistant Forest Ranger had a steady job. "Alton, I'll take it." It was what you might call my first full-time job, even though everything I'd ever done took more than 40 hours a week.

"Okay, Sam. I'll send for you when it's time to report to the Unit. It'll be good to have you back." How about that. Alton could get university graduate foresters, but he wanted me. Of course, I could get a pine seedling to flourish when they couldn't seem to.

In the next several weeks, the Blackwater finished dredging in the canal at Overstreet, headed up the canal through Lake Wimico and the Jackson River, at three miles in length and over 300 feet deep one of the shortest and deepest rivers in the world. From there we sailed into the Apalachicola River. We were pushed and towed by Captain Prior on his Corps of Engineers snag-boat, the US Albany, a paddlewheel river steamer also based in the Ingalls Shipyard drydock at Pascagoula.

The tow consisted of the Blackwater, supporting barges, and our pontoons with the dredge pipelines. The Albany pushed us on the straight runs. On the hairpin river-bends, the swift current of the Apalachicola often pushed us into the river bank. Then the Albany tied up to the bow of the Blackwater and towed us into another straight run. We were towed out of a lot of hairpin riverbends. It was a slow-going chore for Uncle John. I kept cooking and brewing coffee.

Three days out of Apalachicola, Florida, we were only about even with Wewahitchka. At that point our second cook, Jim Peters, fell ill with blood poisoning from picking a pimple on his forehead. We put him on the motor launch and ran him back down the river to a hospital in Apalachicola. Ten days later, the Blackwater reached Fort Benning, Georgia. There we learned that Jim had died. We didn't have penicillin then. If we had, Jim could have survived his infection in that hot, humid climate. But he didn't. I was shocked to see a man with me one day, and gone forever so fast. It was my first encounter with untimely death, up close. It would not be my last.

When I went ashore at Fort Benning, I found out that Alton Hardy wanted me to start work right away. I boarded the Albany for its run down-river to Apalachicola, all 24 hours of it. That was the difference in going downstream versus upstream in that current. The next day I signed on with Alton Hardy as an Assistant Ranger. The Florida Forest Service was started just nine years before in 1928, and Alton's unit was less than two years old. Alton and I worked for Harry Lee Baker, the first State Forester we ever had in Florida. I'd become a sailor, fallen in love with seaplanes, and seen death, but I was most excited about doing a man's job for a man's pay. I was 20 years old. It was September 15, 1937.

RANGER SAM

B. C. Leyenes came to our area from the CCC to survey a site for the forestry tower at Farmdale. B. C. told me about a young man in their camp at Bronson who was very good in forestry. He had finished the CCC training and was doing seasonal fishing on a commercial fishing crew out of San Blas. The St. Joe Forestry Unit was allowed a Ranger helper's position funded under a federal works program, and I needed a helper soon for the fire season — late fall, winter, and early spring.

I went to see the young man, Clyde Spann. When I found Clyde, he and his brother Jake were scrubbing the house floor where they lived in San Blas. They were in the front yard pumping water from a hand pump into a bucket to get water to the floor. I told them to soap up and scrub the floor, and I'd help with the rinsing. When they were ready to rinse, I backed up my forestry fire truck to the front door, handed Clyde the hose, and said, "Now, when I turn on the water pump, you rinse her down and out the back door." Jake and Clyde thought it was a nifty way to get their job done fast without much effort.

Clyde qualified to fill my Ranger's helper position because his commercial fishing work wasn't a permanent job. The first year he worked with me, we patrolled the area from Red Fish Point to Port St. Joe in our fire truck. I had an International Harvester pick-up with a water tank, a pressure pump run off the truck's fan belt, and a 50 foot length of hose with an adjustable nozzle.

On one typical day after my first year, I ate breakfast, left my home in Farmdale, and picked up Clyde in San Blas to start our run. We saw smoke down on the bay in the direction of Belle Isle. Checking that out, we found it was a warming fire the oystermen built on the hill at the Van Strange Point landing. Of course we bought a sack of oysters, then made sure our route took us by the commissary at the Parrish and Allan Turpentine Co. to procure pepper sauce and crackers.

After a lunch of oysters on the half shell, we continued out the Old Farmdale Road to Red Fish Point Road, watching for fires. In the afternoon a lightning squall came up, so we followed along it as it moved through our area. That day the lightning was accompanied by rain that doused the wildfire soon after it started. By dark, nothing was on fire, so I dropped Clyde off at San Blas and went home.

Some lightning fires we put out, and some were put out by rain accompanying the lightning. If we found no fires, some days we repaired abandoned bridges along the old dirt roads for our own use. We did all our own maintenance work on our trucks and equipment.

To be good foresters, we had to have some engineering ability. We were in a country scene where cattlemen ran their cattle on the open range. It was their custom in the winter to burn vast areas of woods to make green grass in the spring for their cattle. The large lumber companies in the early 1900s had cut out the original timber, leaving no seed trees except for culls and what came up without human help. The cattlemen's range fires regularly obliterated sparse woods. These fires burned the "heavy rough," bushes, and woody plants that would otherwise feed a wildfire. Many homeowners burned the woods near their houses to keep wildfire from coming close. Almost nobody had qualms about burning another owner's woodland. It was our job to tell everyone they could no longer burn one another's land and would have to follow the state law to burn their own.

This education of the citizenry was actually public relations. We talked to everyone we could as we patrolled our area and put out fires. In those days we didn't encounter deliberately set arson fires in the woods, so we must have been persuasive. When

B. C. finished his survey, Clyde and I staked out the Farmdale tower site. Then we set stakes in place for telephone poles that carried lines to my house and the turpentiner's house at Overstreet. The day came when we were to meet the man who had contracted with Alton Hardy to cut and haul the logs for telephone poles. The St. Joe Paper Company gave the Forest Service the stumpage on their land along the creeks leading to the Apalachicola River, trees left close to the water when they cut their timber.

I had no idea who the logger was, but I figured I would know a load of 30 foot poles when I saw it. Clyde, however, called the man by name, Curt Eifert. The logger from White City who successfully bid for the contract was a cousin of Clyde's bride, Audrey.

Clyde and I had a plan from the District Office in Panama City for the St. Joe Unit that showed the proposed tower locations and connecting telephone lines. We cleaned up the tower sites, procured the telephone poles, set up the poles, and strung single wire grounded lines on them.

Professional contractors erected the towers at the same time, and we began to hire towermen. Clyde easily qualified for the job at the Farmdale tower. It was his first permanent job. He was 25 years old. The forestry towers were located 18 to 20 miles apart so that even in poor visibility each tower needed sight lines of only 9 or 10 miles to cover the area. Two or three towers sighted on a fire to spot it accurately on the map by triangulation. The towermen called the Rangers to the fires they spotted. Because I was a Ranger, I had a telephone at Mama's and Daddy's house. We could relay around the Forestry Service lines and get a message into Panama City. We could consult Alton Hardy at the District Office or call an ambulance to save a life, as we did once when Mama fell seriously ill. We didn't have electricity yet, but with the telephone we thought we were in fabulous living. The Forest Service was charged with building houses for the towermen and their families on the site of each tower. Soon Clyde and Audrey lived at Farmdale in the house he and I built on the grounds of Clyde's 100 foot tall place of work. I still saw Clyde every day, and soon I met George Toepher and his wife Carol when they visited Audrey and Clyde. George Toepher was a Navy Commander who had been assigned to military duty as a supervisor at Clyde's CCC camp three years before he retired. His military rank was Commander, but in Bay County we all called him "Captain" for his experience at sea. He was a Mustang, a sailor who showed such superior qualities that he was given a commission as a warrant officer or a regular Navy Ensign. He had been an AP, an enlisted Aviation Pilot in the Navy, before he was made an Ensign. I listened to Captain Toepher's stories of life in the Navy and began to envy that life, his world-wide adventures at sea.

FOREST PROTECTION

I came by my enthusiasm for forest conservation from my Daddy's example. He and George Hardy were the two largest cattlemen in my area and the best of fire control citizens. They actively supported what we were doing to reduce fires and develop timber acreage. George Waller and George Hardy were the only two turpentiners left in my area. Waller was another supporter of the Forest Service work in fire control and forest conservation.

Most of the rest of the citizens in the St. Joe Unit didn't set malicious fires. I only averaged one fire a month, and we put them out with them burning five acres or less apiece.

With the decrease in set fires by cattlemen and fewer fire accidents from the turpentiners in my area, Zeke Harding asked Clyde and me if we'd ever had any lightning fires. It was early in our first year at the St. Joe Unit, so we had never seen fires set by lightning. So long as the cattlemen burned the range, lightning couldn't ignite green grass. Zeke told us to expect lightning fires in another year.

Sure enough, when the heavy rough died that winter, we had a fire one afternoon in an almost inaccessible area. The towerman saw the smoke in the midst of an electrical storm. When lightning struck the dead grass and brown bushes, they went up like tinder. If we hadn't had some relief from rain with the lightning, we wouldn't have finished as early as we did that day around 10 p.m.

Carey Whitfield was the Forest Ranger whose territory in north Gulf County abutted mine at Overstreet, along Wetappo Creek and the Intracoastal Waterway. One day he had a fire in his area near the turpentine still at Ring Jaw. He picked up a crew of four men from the still to help him fight it. When the first fire was out, Carey saw smoke further up the dirt road. Just as they got their fire truck back onto the road to go to the next fire, lightning struck with an ear-splitting clap of thunder. The engine stopped, and they piled out of the truck lickety-split onto the ditch bank. After Carey regained his composure, he got back into the truck and stepped on the starter. The truck readily revved up with no signs of a mechanical problem.

Carey called to the crew, "Come on! Let's go put out this other fire."

One of the men said, "No, sir, Mr. Carey. We've done messed with the Lord's work once today, and we don't intend to mess up His work no more." Carey could not persuade them to go with him.

Some rain came soon afterward, so he was able to put the fire out by himself. When Clyde took the tower job, I hired his brother Jake to be my truck helper. Jake had a lame leg — a bout with polio had left him with one leg shorter than the other when it stopped growing. He referred to it as his Ginger Rogers leg, the movie star dancing partner of Fred Astaire. Jake danced well and often. Even having to be careful at times, he could do a lot of work. Zeke Harding challenged me about "hiring a cripple to do a man's job." I hired Jake over Zeke's objection.

Jake was living alone in San Blas. When Jake took the job, my folks had him come live at our house. Jake and I had a fire one afternoon in a remote area. With our hand tools, we had to cut a fire line way up ahead of the wildfire. Then we set a back burn between our fire line and the wildfire. The back burn consumed the heavy rough next to our fire line and widened the line of barren land between burning and unburnt woods. Jake and I worked feverishly for 45 minutes to get the back burn started. In another half hour, the wildfire met the back burn fire and went out. Lucky for us the wildfire hadn't crowned, hadn't gotten so high in the trees that it could waft over the burned ground through the treetops to new woods for its fuel. When a fire crowned, we said it had backfired on us. When Jake and I finally got this fire out, we went back in to the tower to find that Alton Hardy needed us and Carey Whitfield on a large wildfire in Franklin County as quickly as possible.

Alton called in a couple of CCC crews as well. Jake stayed right with me. We ended up fighting the Franklin County fire for three days and nights. Zeke Harding joined us the second day. About 10 p.m. the third day, Zeke came up to me. He said, "Sam, I gotta tell you, you've got some good worker in Jake Spann. Why, he kept up the whole time. He did just great work. He really held out after all, didn't he?" "Yeah, Zeke, he sure did. And he'd fought that bad fire with me early in the day before we got here. I'd say fighting wildfire like Jake has, for four days straight, doesn't hardly mean he's a cripple, now does it?"

LEAVING HOME

T he U. S. Navy ran a recruiting advertisement appealing for Aviation Cadets, and I was not impervious to its message. Through the blue sky streaked an F3F Fighter with fixed landing gear. To the side on a larger scale was a Navy Ensign decked out in dress whites, gold Navy wings, Navy blue shoulder boards with gold star and stripe, white cap with Navy blue band, silver shield, and eagle with bronze-crossed anchors. Not only that, but his arm encircled the shoulders of a brown-eyed brunette with flowing hair. At her feet was the Naval Aviator's green bag. The caption read "Join the Navy, get the $27,000 education, and all this will be yours plus flight pay." In the small print below it read that Aviation Cadet enlistments are open to those who have two years of college.

I hadn't seen any immediate necessity for college before. But now, although my number hadn't been pulled, I was registered for the Draft. I wasn't in a position to be a university graduate forester, and I wasn't eligible to be a Navy Cadet. I needed to do better! I began to save a few dollars out of my pay every month.

On September 1, 1939, Germany invaded Poland so efficiently that the rest of Europe finally noticed the threat of Hitler's regime. On September 3, Britain and France declared war on Germany. Soviet troops took advantage of the Nazi-Soviet nonaggression pact to invade Poland. In April, 1940, Germany attacked Denmark and Norway. In May, Germany successfully invaded France, Belgium, Luxembourg,and the Netherlands. In June, Italy, under the Fascist Benito Mussolini, declared war on Britain and France.

On June 22, 1940, France surrendered to Germany. Nazis goose-stepped down the Champs Elysees in Paris. For a world fresh with memories of World War I, the newsreel pictures from France seemed to stun us into silence.

In August, 1940, I took the bus to the University of Florida for a look-see. The people at the registration office showed me the college catalogue, explained the enrollment procedure, and sent me to see Professor Harold S. Newins, Director of the School of Forestry. Dean Newins's office was on the top floor of the Horticulture Building. On the second floor stairs landing, I met Dr. Muerrel. He put his desk out there because he loved to chat with students as they came and went.

Dr. Muerrel was a noted mycologist who had discovered and classified many species of fungus, both good and bad fungi. He had been head of the New York Botanical Gardens, and was retired from the University of Florida by the time I met him, but he had by no means quit his life's work in the woods and laboratory. From that first day on I always had time to stop and talk with Dr. Muerrel.

On the fourth floor, Dean Newins greeted me warmly with several minutes of talk. He was the first Director of the School of Forestry, then in the Agricultural College. He'd been all over the state many times, attending meetings, making speeches, and generally promoting forestry and the University. The whole time I was with him that first day, he kept the conversation going — where was my home, what kind of forestry work I had done, what my folks did. When I mentioned I was Pasco Davis's son, Dean Newins said, "Yes! I know your dad. I met him at a forestry meeting in Marianna when we were trying to get interest going in fire control for all the counties of Florida and get some money for the Forestry School here. I believe Pasco had George Hardy with him. So you've worked for his son Alton, have you?" I had to catch the bus back home, and Dean Newins kept talking. I finally said, "Thanks so much, Dean. I must go." After about ten more minutes, Dean Newins said, "Well, tell your father I said 'Hello.' I enjoyed meeting him. I like to talk with the down to earth people I meet in West Florida."

Dean Newins talked a lot, and he said a lot. That day he told me about the CLO House, the Cooperative Living Organization, saying it was a nice place to live and most inexpensive. It had begun with two country boys from West Florida rooming together, doing their own cooking in a small apartment off campus. It sounded like my kind of place.

LEAVING THE PORT ST. JOE FORESTRY UNIT

My last day of work with the St. Joe Unit ended on a Sunday afternoon. What could go wrong? First, fire broke out that afternoon in Alton Hardy's territory. Of course I went to his aid. We put the fire out about 9 p.m. That was okay. I could still catch the bus on time the next day for Gainesville and the University. Alton asked as I started to leave if I could meet a transport truck from Lake City that was bringing a tractor and fire line plow to begin fire line plowing. Over the last three years, my helpers and I had cleared enough firelines so that a Caterpillar crawler tractor and a Settlemire four-disc plow could get back in the woods to plow connecting ten-foot fire breaks. The transport with this tractor on it was due at the Belle Isle School building by 9 a.m., and my bus left Panama City at 2 p.m.

I would meet the transport, then leave the Forest Service truck at the district office in Panama City, catch my bus, and go. Sure, I could do that. At 9 a.m. I was at Belle Isle to meet the transport. I had my suitcase packed and with me in my truck in case the transport was a little late. Nothing ever works like it's supposed to. An hour passed, no transport and tractor. Another hour, nothing. I was in a bind. Two o'clock came and no tractor. I was ready to go, and I couldn't. By 3 p.m. I was furious, foaming at the bits, getting madder every minute. Finally, here came the transport and tractor. I told George Gary, the driver, how thoroughly put out I was that he was horribly late, and that I'd missed the bus to Gainesville. When he could get a word in edgewise, he said, "You want to go to Gainesville? I can take you to Lake City if you're ready to go now." Was I ever! I called the District office from the transport truck to make different arrangements now that it was so late in the day. By then the Forest Service was moving away from the telephone lines that linked towers, rangers, turpentine stills, and sawmills. Communications were being upgraded to a 2-way radio system. George Gary's transport truck had a receiver and a transmitter already. George and I left the tractor at Belle Isle for the time being. I gave him the map, showed him where to start plowing the fire line, and handed him my Forest Service truck key. He said he'd be glad to get the truck back to Alton Hardy for me. I grabbed my suitcase, boarded the transport truck, and George drove me to Lake City 250 miles away and only 50 miles from Gainesville. From Lake City I hitch-hiked in the middle of the night to Gainesville.

George turned around and went back to Belle Isle, a total of 500 miles out of his way. He was a late son-of-a-gun, but he was a good friend to me that day after all.

THE CLO
HOUSE

It was September 1940 when I drew out all my savings and enrolled as a freshman in the University of Florida, the first of my family to enter a regular session of college. I wanted to get in two years at the University and qualify to fly those beautiful seaplanes. If the Army was my fate, I wanted to finish Reserve Officer Training (ROTC) and go in on an officer's commission. In order to get a good paying job in the woods, I wanted to finish a for-estry degree.

I signed up for ROTC, both motorized and horse-drawn Field Artillery, a load of introductory freshman courses, and one class in forestry. I was a little fish in a big pond. I could still be drafted. On September 22, 1940, Japan successfully pushed into French Indochina, the nation later to be called Viet Nam. My first year of college, President Roosevelt and Congress began a lend-lease program with Great Britain. We lent materials to the government of King George VI and Prime Minister Winston Churchill. They would return them to us at some unspecified future date, or at that unspecified time they would make lease payments for all the time they had the ships and arms. It was a transparent ploy, but it got past the isolationists in our nation. If we didn't supply Great Britain, Germany would destroy the British Navy and rule the North Atlantic right up to our shores. The National Guard was called into the Army. Captain Toepher went back into the Navy as a Commander.

In those days, the State militia were called up first. Draft inductions began in the United States for the rest of us young men. It was supposed to last only a year. I didn't especially want to be drafted, but the short time limit didn't make sense. You couldn't win a war in just one year. As soon as I had registered in the freshman class, I went to the CLO House and signed in with them. Those first two apartment mates had been joined by two more country boys from West Florida their second year. Then more came, and they rented a whole house. The University decided it was a good undertaking and helped the CLO organize in perpetuity.

Dr. Joseph R. Fulk, a retired English professor, and his wife, Nellie Swanson Fulk, lived in a nice brick home near one of the CLO rental houses. He thought the CLO was such a good idea that he gave them a trust deed for the house and garage on his property in the 200 block of North Washington Street (now NW 15th Street).

In addition, Dr. Fulk willed his own home to the CLO at his or his wife's death, whichever came last. When Mrs. Fulk died first, Dr. Fulk moved to another place and deeded his brick residence in trust to the CLO. He lived for several more years, and I met him at some of the CLO business meetings while I was there.

I got through my first year at the University of Florida with the help of my three sophomore roommates at the CLO House — Joe Busby and Bill McCown from Lake County, and Paul Sims from Marianna. Their fellowship was necessary to my academic standing. College wasn't the soft snap high school had been. I was five years older than Joe, Paul, and Bill. All three tried to keep me straight during the year.

At that time there were 80 of us in the CLO. We owned Dr. Fulk's brick house, the garage apartment to the house, a white frame house, and a brown painted house, all in the 224 block of North Washington Street. In addition, we rented a two story house on the back end of a lot just south of the white house. We used the first floor of the rented house as the kitchen and dining room and the second floor as a bunk room. We elected officers among ourselves and formed committees for property upkeep, kitchen management, food purchasing, personnel management — everything that made us self-supporting. Our monthly bill for each student was $18.50 in 1940-41. By the end of the 1941-42 academic year, we had to charge $23.50 a month to stay out of the red.

My three roommates and I lived in the back corner room of the two story house, getting along comfortably, having no problems with each other. I was the freshman, they were the upperclassmen. They had a rat paddle but never used it to any extent on me. I was five years older than each of them, and they, perhaps reluctantly, gave me a little respect.

One day my roommates decided that being away from our mothers' supervision, we should clean up the room. Which meant that I, the freshman rat, was to do the cleaning. After a couple of hours of me sweeping, dusting, and mopping, Bill and Paul decided to show the juniors in the rooms above the kitchen how hard I was being worked. Joe didn't know they were going to do that. He felt sorry for me by then, so he took over the last bit of mopping. He mopped, and I sat tuckered out on the bed. Bill and Paul came back with some mean wielders of the rat paddle, including Pat Hunter, Woodrow "Coon Bottom" Glen, and Johnny Mac Brown. Everyone was supposed to see how Joe, Bill, and Paul were treating their lowly freshman. They saw Joe mopping and me lazing on the bed. I was whacked with the paddle real good for that. In fact, they darn near used the paddle on Joe.

That cleanup revealed to us that we had 32 pairs of dirty socks under the corner bunk. For months we had gotten a pair of socks dirty and thrown them there. No one knew which ones he owned, so we washed all of them and gave each of us eight pairs of socks. Dean Newins was right — the CLO House was my kind of place.

LEAVING
FARMDALE

The summer of 1941, I went home to Farmdale for the last time. The U. S. Army was taking Daddy's homestead on East St. Andrew's Bay for Tyndall Field. In those days, if the military wanted something, they just took it by government right of eminent domain and paid us what they said it was worth. Daddy rushed to beat the deadline for getting his free-range cattle out of the area. I went right out of college to a horse's back, from early morning to late at night. It took us weeks to round up cattle and drive them around the head of the Bay. There we took them across the ferry at Overstreet to Allanton, to go to a pasture that was the old homestead of his Aunt Nin Stone Kirvin. Daddy sold some of the cattle to buy this property from Mary Jane Stone Kirvin, his Aunt Nin.

The ferry was a flat bottom barge-like craft. It moved along a cable stretched from one side of the canal to the other. The ferryman used an oak limb with a notch cut into one end to go over the cable. He grabbed the cable with the limb. From the bow of the boat he walked back to the stern as he pulled on the cable with the notched limb. When he got back there, he took the limb back to the bow and did it again, thereby making the ferry move across the water. The cable fit through a groove in the rail of the ferry so that the boat didn't float away downstream. The cable was wound up on a reel on one bank of the Inland Waterway. When the ferry was off the banks, the cable stretched taut across the water. When the ferry rested on a bank awaiting another passenger, the cable was unreeled to rest slack at the bottom of the Waterway. Ships could get past the cable when the ferry wasn't crossing the water.

Daddy and my brothers had enough cowboys to keep the herd

corralled on each side of the ferry landing. The ferry's load limit was three cars. Model T Fords in those days were about 1500 pounds, so we could force only about 20 head of cattle at a time onto the boat for each crossing. We had to stop to let other boats pass. It took a full day to get all the cattle across.

Daddy rode our horse "Prince" that day. Prince was a fine, smooth, fast-walking, easy-riding horse who could turn on a dime and give you back eight cents change. We borrowed Uncle George's horse "Duck" for me to ride. Uncle George's children usually rode Duck, but they made him run and gallop. Duck knew nothing about walking smoothly and fast. I couldn't rein him in well when rounding up the cattle. We rode these horses every day, beginning before daylight and going on into the night.

I was mighty frustrated with Duck all those hours. I was in a patch of timber way down the Gulf of Mexico beach near Crooked Island Point when I spotted eight steers that had been eluding us for days. They saw me and struck out in a run toward the point. Of course, that was opposite the direction I wanted them to go. Duck and I sped up to head them off. I picked out the way I wanted and urged Duck on. I was reining him to go to the right of a big pine tree when, too close for comfort, Duck decided to turn and go to the left, nearly throwing me off into the tree. I was pulling leather trying to get Duck under control. Finally I reined him out of the timber and onto the top of a Gulf beach sand dune ridge. Right there I planned to get rid of this dumpy little horse as soon as I could.

After running along the ridge a bit, we came up fast on a break in the ridge where the wind currents cut a swath right across it. Too late to stop this unruly horse, I saw the twelve foot drop. I let him go. Duck sailed off into the bottom of the swath with me on him. He landed on all four feet evenly and solid, with me still on him. He stood there quietly. I got off, cuddled his head in my arms and cheek and said, "Oh, you sweet little cow pony!" I led him out of the swath to the edge of the sand hill. He was okay. I was okay. We were ahead of the steers.

That day we drove the steers home, seven miles away. Thereafter I had more patience with Duck. In less than a week I taught him to walk smoothly and fast. He learned how to let me rein him in. That summer we got most of Daddy's cattle herd together and across the ferry. I learned an important lesson about stupid creatures who'd never had a chance to do something right the first time. It took me a lot longer to give up on someone after that summer with Duck, the little cow pony.

TYNDALL FIELD

In late August of 1940, I left to the others the rest of the job of driving Daddy's cattle onto the Allanton pasture. I moved to Panama City to live with my sister Eloise and her husband, Gene Cain, while I worked as a checker for building construction at Tyndall Field for $135 a month. I rode to work with a couple of friends who helped me get the job.

Everything was going on at Tyndall, at a quick pace and on a large scale. There were a number of contractors with their crews doing their jobs on a cost plus basis. My friends and I checked to see that the government got a fair shake. We rode horses down through the woods to the various jobs to see how the work was going on each one. My job was to check the crews as to how many men and how many hours they worked, then to see if that jibed with what the contractors were turning in. We were supposed to see that the government got what it paid for from all these projects.

Tyndall Field runways were built by clearing the land and burning the uprooted trees as trash. The crews scooped out all the mud from the swamps down to the sand bottom, then filled the area back in with sand hauled in by dump trucks and pushed in with bulldozers. In other areas they built hangars, roads, office buildings, living quarters, houses — everything all at once. The old Florida piney woods were reshaped.

My generation hadn't had secure work in more than ten years, and we were hungry to do anything we could for steady pay. People were glad to have a job, any job. We worked hard; we were grateful. There was lots of work to be done, and at last there was money to pay us to do it.

My first year at the University of Florida I had lived at the CLO, bought books, paid tuition and fees, had a little (a very little) recreation — for a total expense of $302.98. At the Tyndall Field job, I made enough money to keep me in college for my second year. I had to pay a late fee of $5 when I enrolled at Gainesville, but I figured that with four weeks of paid work, I had a net gain of $130 from this one job.

My home went under for this government project. In the 1930s, my grandparents had been buried in the Farmdale cemetery among all the marked graves going back to the early 1800s. Some of the smaller graves were known only by empty shells put face-down in patterns to mark where the bodies were buried. In the 1940s, their graves became part of a demolition range of Tyndall Field. All the buildings in Farmdale were eventually destroyed. All that was left of our home was the big tree in our front yard. All that was left of Farmdale were the foundations of the schoolhouse and the post office.

The cemetery remained on the rise at the bend of the bayou. The old pine trees around the cemetery still whispered in the wind to the graves. The water slid peacefully around the foot of the sand hill that held those who never left their home.

US Blackwater dredging the Apalachicola River

Sam and the other mess cooks

Sam hitchhiking home for draft deferment, Sept.1941

Cadet Sam poses on a display plane at Georgia pre-flight school

Above:
Sam's forest ranger's truck

Right: Forest lookout tower
in Farmdale

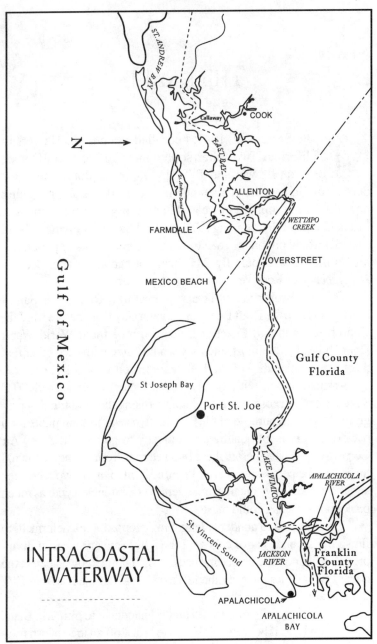

Waterway covered by the Blackwater with Sam aboard as cook

THE DRAFT

In late September, 1941, I enrolled again in the University of Florida. Two other sophomores in the CLO House, Branson Brewer and T. T. Hatton, took pilot training just outside of Gainesville. This made me comfortable about signing up for it for my sophomore year. I hadn't forgotten the seaplanes. I took Civilian Pilot Training (CPT) at Carl Stengel's Flying School, a small airfield out on the road to Archer. Three weeks of pilot training let me know I could fly. My dream of becoming an officer — Army, Navy, or Reserve — was looking closer.

Then in October my turn came: "Greetings" from Uncle Sam. I hurried home to the Draft Board in Panama City to go before Mr. J. E. Churchwell and Mr. Fletcher Black, both of them World War I Doughboys. I was almost sure they would agree with each other that there was nothing they could do to defer me only for college.

I armed myself with the Navy Cadet requirements, the ROTC Statement of Purpose, and the flyer advertising the pilot training program. The stated purpose of CPT in the flyer was to train pilots for a backlog reservoir of qualified pilots ready to go into the Army Air Corps. When I went before these two veterans from my home town, I turned on the persuasive charm. I poured it on to those two men deep and thick, like heavy cream from a Jersey cow, mingled with as much backwoods wit as I could muster.

They seemed to ponder at length my proposal for a deferment to finish my second year of college. I thought I saw grimaces of disapproval. After no little time, Mr. Black said, "I don't know a man in the county with better integrity than Pasco Davis. Let me read that CPT thing again."

With all the poise of a scared rabbit I handed it to him. Mr. Black read it slowly, as if he were thinking. He broke off an inch of ash from his cigar and spit his tobacco juice into the highly polished brass spittoon, a perfect bull's eye without any mess on either side of the rim. He looked over his glasses to Mr. Churchwell.

"Well, it seems to me Sam, here, has been in training for some time in the Civilian Military Training Camp in the past, and now he's in college with ROTC and pilot training. He's already soloed the Tandem Cub and knows he can fly. So if it's okay with you, J. E., then it's okay with me."

"I was about to voice what you just said, Fletch, and I think we wouldn't go wrong by deferring him for six months."

I took what I could get. With six months grace I knew I would still be short of the two years of college requirement for the Navy Cadets, short of advanced ROTC status, and short of finishing Civilian Pilot Training. It wasn't long enough to get through the next eight more months of school, but it would have to do. The two old gentlemen signed my paper, and I thanked them graciously as I stepped out of their office.

It was 3:15 in the afternoon, and I had to get back to Gainesville, but not before I went to James' Cleaners to see Mr. James' brunette daughter with the big brown eyes. She had just come from Bay High, where she graduated in 1940, with a transcript of her records for her application to Army Nurse Training. She asked me what I was doing there, as she expected I should be in Gainesville. I told her I hadn't come by to pick up any cleaning, but I thought it most necessary that we go across the street to Brewer's Drug Store for an ice cream soda before I got on the road for Gainesville again.

Over the ice cream and seltzer, I told her my Draft number had come up, and I had just received a deferment from the Board. Her gracious manner turned to disgust. She looked somewhat like a mashed potato sandwich when you pour a glass of icewater on it.

She did consent to drive me out to the north end of Harrison Avenue, where I stepped out to thumb my way back to school. As she was turning around, a hardware salesman from Baird's in Gainesville stopped and picked me up. He recognized my orange and blue Florida Rat Cap; he asked how I was doing.

I told him that I had just come from the Draft Board wanting a nine months' deferment and gotten six. My brown-eyed brunette, the future Army Nurse, thought I was a PFC Draft dodger. I felt like I'd been to the cleaners after all.

THE WAR IN GAINESVILLE, FLORIDA

The first priority of all Civilian Pilot Training students was flying; my other studies were a distant second in importance. The University administration encouraged this attitude. We had standing permission to skip classes because weather conditions dictated flying schedules. I spent so much time flying that I couldn't catch up in Basic Math, so I dropped it that fall.

All of Europe and half of Asia were at war. We were continually given new regulations on flying. Jacksonville Naval Air Station began intensively flying cadets.

Dr. Walker, an engineering professor, taught aircraft maintenance and piloting. On December 7, 1941, he took 11 of us CPT students to Jacksonville Airport to the Civil Aeronautics Administration Control Center. We returned late to his Gainesville home. That evening, all our lives changed. Like everyone of my generation, I remember exactly where I was when I heard the news.

Japan had bombed Pearl Harbor and Guam. They had attacked our own territories. For security reasons, we didn't know at the time how much of our Pacific Fleet was devastated that day. But we knew enough to come together behind President Roosevelt. I knew then, before his speech to Congress on December 8, 1941, that it meant war for me. I didn't think about dying young.

The order came to stop all civilian flying. My pilot training was put on hold. Before Christmas, another order came to check all pilot trainees for citizenship and issue those who qualified a card to allow them to finish flying. That semester I had soloed, flown acrobatics, flown solo cross country, passed the ground work, and received my two credits for the course. But I hadn't gone far enough to be issued a Private Pilot's license.

By January, 1942, I had dropped too many courses to have enough credits to keep me in school, pilot training was still on hold, and I would be drafted in two months. I could almost see buck private, drawing $21 a month pay with a rifle in my hand and a pack on my back.

But my luck hadn't run out.

First, for the Spring 1942 semester, the University of Florida instituted new courses to help with the war effort. Meteorology and Celestial Navigation entered the curriculum, each as a three hour credit. I had completed those subjects already in pilot training, so I signed up for the two courses, earned the University credits with little extra work, and reinstated my good academic standing.

Second, about this time a Navy flight instructor and his student/cadet landed in Gainesville for a Coke and couldn't get his SNJ started. Instructors commonly landed these low wing monoplane fighter trainers at Stengel's school, but it was uncommon for them to get stranded. Carl called a bunch of us guys over to help start the SNJ with his bungee starter.

The bungee starter was a large, long, elastic rubber rope — a bungee — with a leather pouch in the middle. The pouch fit over the top of the plane's propeller. Carl pulled the propeller backwards to keep it from flipping over, while an equal number of students ran out with the two ends of the bungee. Each group ran at an angle from each other, to the utmost stretch of the bungee. Then Carl tripped up the propeller. The tension of the bungee snapped it forward, turning over the engine. The pilot meantime used the choke and throttle to start the engine as it turned over. The reason we students ran out at an angle was that when the propeller came over and the engine started, the leather cup and the bungee would be thrown between us instead of at us.

Our prodigious efforts didn't start the SNJ that day. The Naval Air Station at Jacksonville couldn't send a mechanic to fix the plane until the next day. Nothing would do but that the instructor and his cadet spend the night at my Cooperative Living Organization House. That evening he told us we could get someone to come over to Gainesville to give a recruit information talk if we wrote him that at least 35 of us were interested.

We posted the information on bulletin boards throughout the University, got about 40 students interested, and notified Dean Beaty so that he could write to the recruiter.

A full Lieutenant came and gave us a most flowery talk. He told us we could sign up, get selected by the Aviation Cadet Board in Atlanta, forget about being drafted, come back, finish our two years of college, go to Pre-Flight together, and name ourselves the Florida Fighting Gators Squadron.

My Draft Board had been generous with me in doing their distasteful job. It was necessary to call up young men to go to war. But I was young and selfish. At the time I felt I could do all this and thumb my nose at the dog-face Draft Board. So on March 2, 1942, I was selected in Atlanta as an Aviation Cadet. I was made a Second Class Seaman, put on inactive duty, and sent back to school to finish my two years.

That day Atlanta received word that the Navy had just dropped the two years college requirement. I was told that I could go in right then or finish that year at the University and go to Pre-Flight school in June. I decided to be smart as well as patriotic. I signed up as a Second Class Seaman awaiting Pre-Flight Training in June, 1942.

NEW PLACES

I fought World War II between my sophomore and junior years of college, but not before I took off two weeks to see my family.

The speckled trout were biting so well the summer of 1942 in East St. Andrew's Bay that I caught a mess of fish every other day. Uncle Mood and I caught strings of trout that dangled in the water when I stood up in our boat and held one end straight over my head. My Mama's fried fish, hush puppies, sweet iced tea, and big sliced onions were almost conducive to an urge to go over the hill.

For the duration of World war II, Mama saw all three of us boys on active duty. Jim served in the Merchant Marine, Carl in the Coast Guard, and I in the Navy. For years she had no clear idea where we were on the world's seas.

I soldered our three services insignia to a gold bar pin and hung from it a cloisonne rectangle of three blue stars on a field of white edged in red. I gave the pin to Mama to wear. I wanted her to stay a Blue Star mother, not have to endure the tragedy of changing a star to Gold on the death of a son.

On June 25, 1942, I reported to Navy Pre-Flight School at the University of Georgia in Athens. No one at Pre-Flight knew anything about the recruit talk of a Florida or any other "Fighting Gator" Squadron. Two-thirds of the University of Florida recruits from the talk at my CLO House were in the Second Battalion with me. Four more Gators showed up at Pre-Flight in the Third Battalion. At the end of Pre-Flight, our group of Gators were further dispersed by our various assignments to the four Elimination and Primary Flight bases.

Five of us University of Florida recruits were sent to Dallas,

Texas, after Pre-Flight training. Four of us reached Corpus Christi Naval Air Station in Texas together: Buck Battle, Oscar Braddock, Ed Finlayson, and me. Of course, being Floridians, we were not sent to Pensacola for Flight training. The logic of that decision escapes me to this day.

I was introduced to the N3N, a biplane trainer manufactured at the Naval Aircraft Factory in Philadelphia. It had so many mishaps that we called it the "Yellow Peril." There were also a number of Stearman Trainers in Dallas which looked much the same as the Yellow Perils except that they had more power and a steerable tail wheel.

In Dallas, the first thing I noticed was no more bungee starters at Lew Footes Field. The Yellow Perils and the Steerman Trainers had inertia starters. To start one, I took out the stowable crank and attached it to the starter. I turned the starter flywheel until it was revving up, usually winding it 18 turns or so. Then I quickly jumped into the cockpit, opened the throttle, and pulled out the choke. When the engine first fired, I pushed in the choke and caught the engine with the throttle to keep it running. If I couldn't keep the engine running at this point, I'd do the procedure all over again.

It was still a step up from the bungee.

The second thing I noticed in Dallas was that all the planes had airspeed indicators that worked. Fancy that! In one of the planes at Stengel's flight school, we had to judge our airspeed after takeoff from the hum of the crosswires that braced the struts of the wings. The slip-stream of air passing over the wires played a tone similar to the smooth, nice sound of a bow on a fiddle string when it's properly tightened. A high tone meant high airspeed. A medium pitch meant ample airspeed to stay airborne. A sound like pulling a bow across a loose string indicated stalling speed, too low to remain aloft.

At Stengel's school we used mechanical airspeed indicators, but we also listened for the tones in the wires. I wasn't accustomed to depending solely on mechanical indicators. At the end of every hop in Dallas, I did an aerobatic routine the Navy way — split "S," slow rolls, snap rolls, loops, and immelmans. One day my instructor, Ensign Roe, flew with me to see how I was doing. Everything was okay except for the snap rolls. I came out of them headed about 30 degrees off the original heading. Roe told me to practice the rolls until I held the same heading, consistently.

On my next solo trip, I flew to 6,000 feet and did snap rolls the whole period. When I was satisfied I had perfected them, I looked at my watch to find I was 10 minutes overdue at the field. There was no time left to do all the aerobatic routine. I pushed the nose down at cruising throttle and high-tailed it toward home.

A few minutes later, I glanced down for some reason. I found my seat belt wasn't buckled. Hadn't been buckled the whole hop. The snap rolls all period had kept me in my seat by centrifugal force. Had I done my whole routine, I would have fallen out of the open cockpit while upside down.

I felt a chill, wondering how I had lost track of the time, wondering why I hadn't done my aerobatic routine that day. I also wondered about Mama's idea that a guardian angel watched over each of her children.

After much practice, I finally corrected my snap rolls to come out on my original heading. On my check ride with the instructor, Ensign Roe gave me an arrow pointing up after my name on the flight board. I made it all the way through Primary Flight flying without any down checks.

Some of my friends weren't so good at it. Even after spending extra time, Al Duvernay from New Orleans had a down check prior to his solo flying. He had to go before the Old Man, our Navy slang for the commander of the base. Rather than a dismissal from training, Al received more time and was assigned to Lt. "Red Horse" Myers, a seasoned instructor.

All of us were anxious for Al to do well and stay in the program. I came in early from my own flight to find him standing around in the hangar and looking long-faced. "Well Al, how'd you do?"

"Frankly I don't know 'cause Red Horse is in the office talking to the Old Man."

That didn't sound so good. Al could be dismissed from training by the base commander.

"Al, what happened?"

"Look here, Sam."

Al pulled me around to a Yellow Peril with a bent prop and a bent fairing on the landing strut. Red Horse had found out Al wasn't yet able to hold a straight course on takeoff, so he took the controls to show Al how to steer the plane by walking the rudder down the runway back and forth.

As they were climbing, Red Horse was still moving the plane back and forth to show Al how to guide it. When they had just climbed above the airfield, they heard a terrific noise. Sticks flew all over the air around them. Red Horse had plowed through a mesquite "tree."

There was only one little scrawny mesquite in all of five miles around Lew Footes Field, and the instructor flew right through the top of it. Al was reprieved for a while longer.

One day the weather was so bad in Dallas that we were sent out to fly cross country below 6,000 feet instead. My instructor that day was Jerry Flint, and we had a ball. Jerry flew our Yellow Peril at low altitude up a creek bed that fed into the Trinity River. We took every crook and turn, and I looked up to see the tops of the cypress trees along the banks.

Another one of the planes landed in a cow pasture when their engine cut out. Red Horse flew a Yellow Peril through the doors of an open hangar.

I guess we were a little bit crazy, the way we flew that day. But you had to be a little crazy, or be young and think you were immortal to go into Japan alone. You had to be a little crazy to bomb their installations, or to escort bombers to their drop zones, or to go in to rescue pilots down in the water. By the end of 1942, I believed I had everything I needed for my grand adventure: top-notch flying skills and a guardian angel gaining work experience.

NEW FACES

I went into the Navy in the days after radio and before television. I wasn't shocked to find a world out there unlike my own. But the differences among people from other areas of the U.S.A. were still distinct enough to notice.

One day in our barracks a group of us were in a bull session with one fellow telling a wild tale about Bridgeport, Connecticut. A Southerner asked where that was.

"Why you dumb Southern farmer, don't you know where Bridgeport is? How could you be so dumb?"

Hiram Kelley, the Southerner, answered, "Well, fellow, do you know where Bonifay is?"

"No."

"Well, fellow, you are the dumbest thing in the world if you don't know where Bonifay is."

Well, I knew about Bonifay. It's a small country town in West Florida about 50 miles north of Panama City. Kelley and I became good friends that day.

Charades was a popular game, and I was sought after because I knew a lot of Florida places with names no one else had heard before. They were also the devil to act out, be-cause I was partial to Indian names of many syllables. I could always summon up a "Talla-hassee," an "Apalachicola," or a "Choctawhatchee." My favorite in the right company was "Kissimmee." The first time I encountered Texans was in Navy Chapel. The Chaplains asked us to identify ourselves by our home states as they named them in turn. We raised our hands as the states were called out in alphabetical order. When the Chaplain called out "Texas," nothing would do but for the Texans to jump up and yell a raucous "Yeeaaah-Hooo!"

I thought they were indeed a bunch of yahoos. I modified my opinion later to "unique." After Dallas I was assigned to Corpus Christi,

"Corpus" to everyone who's ever lived there. The wind in Corpus blows constantly at about 7 to 15 knots. I could always tell a country girl from a city girl in Corpus: when a puff of wind blew, the country girl grabbed her dress around the hem at her knees; the city girl reached up and hung onto her hat. It was a great place to fly. I had a lot more to learn there.

TEXAS WOMEN

Navy people seem to judge a place by the way local folks treat us on liberty. We say there are only two good bases in all the Navy: the one you just shipped out from; and the one you're going to next. I always considered myself slow to operate well on liberty in Corpus.

One weekend, Oscar Braddock and I stayed downtown at the Nueces Hotel, as the room rate was $3 a night for each of us. We met a bunch of young ladies at a night club the first night out, and were emboldened by some success. When Braddock and I got up the next day, we went down to the hotel lobby and wrangled an invitation from the girls who worked the switchboard to go to their apartment for Cokes and hamburgers. I called one of them "Yankee" because she came down to work in Corpus from north of the Mason Dixon line.

When the girls got off work, Braddock and I hired a taxi to go to their apartment near Spohn Hospital, the main hos-pital in Corpus then. We ordered hamburgers, a couple of quarts of beer, and some Cokes, from the Hospital Grill in the neighborhood.

While we were waiting for our food order, Oscar and I noticed a woman, a wee bit older than we were, sitting alone drinking a beer. We eyed her up, but both of us being somewhat backward, didn't strike up a conversation with her. She eyed us up also, but we were timid, we had dates already, and we didn't speak. After awhile she finished and walked out.

When our order was ready, we walked out and saw the woman down the street a short distance. She slowed down. We sped up. She grasped the overhanging limb of one of those little mesquite "trees," pulling it forward as she walked. When we came up, she let go of the mesquite limb, and it snapped back in our faces. That dulled our backwardness and stimulated our interest, so we finally spoke to her.

"You boys like to party?" she asked.

"Well sure, Ma'am." That ma'am didn't seem to please her, but she went on anyway.

"I'm having a party at my house real soon, and I'd like to have you boys drop by. Why don't you call me when you're not so busy? I'll give you directions. My name is Helen Berry, and I'm in the phone book."

"Yeah, we'll do that." No "ma'am" this time.

By later in the week, neither Braddock nor I had any luck with calls for dates. Braddock got a phone book and looked up Helen Berry. She was listed as "Mrs. Helen Berry," but that didn't phase us. She told us where her house was, we were welcome to come, and there would be other girls there, too.

It was Wednesday night when we made these arrangements. Thursday morning, the Navy Base revamped and stepped up our flight training schedule. We went on an eight day week. The base would fly every day. The cadets would be grouped in eight divisions. One division would be on liberty for two days while the other seven flew. Braddock was in another division than mine. I pulled liberty for the coming Saturday and Sunday.

Helen answered the door that weekend.

"Come in and make yourself at home."

Then she busied herself elsewhere, to leave me with an odd collection of her boarders. One of them was a beautiful nurse, from whom I wanted to wheedle a kiss before getting back to base.

After a great while, Helen came in from the kitchen with a broom, as if she were sweeping the floor. Then she held it in front of her and began to step to the music. As she danced with the broom, she said, "My boyfriend won't dance with me so I have to dance with a broom."

I was dancing with the nurse by then, and it was getting late. I decided to call a taxi.

Taxi service in Corpus was highly overtaxed, especially on Saturday night. It took an hour and twenty minutes for a taxi to get there for me. I got tired of waiting. I said, "Look, he's not coming. I'm going to go on ahead back to base. I can hitchhike faster than this."

Helen said, "No, the taxi hasn't come." "Well, I doubt he's coming, so I'll walk down to Six Points and catch the bus."

"You can't do that, because the taxi driver would get mad if he showed up at this address and didn't get a fare. They'd never send a taxi out here, and all the people renting a room from me are working people. They have to depend on good relations with the taxi people."

Well, I was a working man. I hitchhiked a lot of places. I knew what it was like to have to depend on buses and taxis. I stayed and tried to mend the bad relations I'd caused at Helen's "party."

Finally I was back at the base safe and sound. Braddock asked, "How'd you make out?"

"Frankly, I don't know." The next day I went back to town with Al DuVernay who had come in to Corpus and over to our barracks. We took the bus into town for a fish dinner. We were eating red fish at the Nixon Cafe on Leopard Street, just above the bluff in downtown Corpus, not even thinking about girls until we saw a white Lincoln convertible with two women in it drive up the hill on Leopard Street. We stood up in the front plate glass panel and waved to them. They waved back, swiftly swerved into the curb, got out of that flashy car, and came in to join us.

A few minutes later Russell and Bradley, two other cadets I knew, came in. Maude Price, the owner of the convertible, had been partying with these guys. We finished eating, wondering what to do, when Maude said she could find another girl or two, and we should go out to her home.

Bradley first had to check out of the Plaza Hotel across the street, so everyone accompanied him there. While Russell and Bradley packed their clothes, Maude emptied all the part bottles of whiskey into one and put all the unopened Cokes in her bag. She said to me, "You know, I have a good income, a white convertible, and plenty of red stamps for gas, and I don't see why I can't get one of these young men, do you?"

"Maude, I can think of only one more thing they'd want."

"Well, I probably got plenty of that too."

"Oh."

We picked up three of Maude's girlfriends and spent the rest of the evening at Maude's, a big house in the center of a horse-shoe shaped drive with rooming cottages on each side of it. I remember Blanche Valley from that evening; she was a standout. You could never forget her, coal black hair, tanned complexion, dark brown eyes, pretty smile, and excellent figure.

It was a delightful adventure. Maude took all of us cadets back to the base that night.

My delight didn't last the week. Oscar Braddock went to see Helen Berry on his next liberty the following Tuesday night. When he returned he asked me, "What in heaven did you do last Saturday night?"

I had to confess, "I don't know."

It had been a confusing week. I concluded that doing aviation maneuvers was much easier than coping with Texas women on liberty.

THE FIFTH
WOMAN

I was a young man in my twenties and there was a war on. I didn't feel the necessity to have a wife before I went off to invade Japan, but in peace it would have been time for me to settle down. Accordingly, there was an important woman about to come into my life.

On that first night at Helen Berry's I had set my bottle of whiskey down amidst a half dozen others on a large coffee table made entirely of sections of plate glass. Glancing around, I was totally surprised at the scene before me and wondered if I ought to be there.

A teenaged boy and a younger child were playing records on a Victrola. A couple in their mid-twenties with a young baby were sitting at the coffee table. At the end of the table was a 4-F type, a civilian not physically fit for military service, about 30 years of age. He didn't count in those days. My eyes focused like magic on a rocking chair to the side of the room in which sat this beautiful nurse. I set to finding out that her name was Mary Lona Forgy.

I didn't go unnoticed by Mary Lona either. She said later she saw a black-haired "gorgeous" flyer in his Navy whites, catnip to the ladies. She thought my brown eyes seemed like a western Indian. I looked a little lost to her. Small wonder.

She decided she had to get that cap out of my hand before I fled the premises. She said I was the best-looking thing she had ever seen in Helen's rooming house. Navy whites do wonders on a man.

Mary Lona had been required to go into nurse's training by her family rather than attend college, even though they sent her older brother to Texas A&I in Kingsville. After completing two of the required three years of training in San Antonio, she was called home to nurse her father through his last illness, Lou Gehrig's disease. After he died, they decided she should be closer to home. They sent her to repeat her training and finish nursing school in Corpus.

Home was a farm on a fertile plain between Odem, Edroy, and Sinton, Texas, in the neighboring county. Mary Lona grew up there as the middle child between her brothers Paul and Ernest. Now she was back in Corpus by choice. She frankly wanted to be where she would meet and date a lot of men. Providentially, the naval air station was less than 40 miles from her widowed mother.

Mary Lona was engaged to Army Sgt. Theodore Ressler, or semi-engaged depending on what part of the story is told at which time. She had nursed him at the Veterans' Hospital in Dallas and was genuinely fond of him. But she was also practical about her rules for dating: "Never go steady until you get engaged, and never get engaged until you've set the wedding date."

Lucky for me! Their engagement was for an indefinite time. The Army man was on duty elsewhere the day I wan-dered into Helen Berry's parlor.

I recall that someone put on a record, so I took the opportunity to ask this beautiful nurse to dance. Mary Lona remembered that she queried me about what music I liked and put the record on herself. It was her intention that I should dance with her. Of course I asked this shapely brunette with the huge blue eyes to dance with me. That's what handsome flyers and pretty nurses do when there's a War on, you know. I assumed Mary Lona was one of the girls Helen had hinted would be at her place when Braddock and I met her outside the Hospital Grill. Mary Lona wasn't ever one of Helen's girls, as became evident in Helen's pique with me later that evening. Mary Lona was renting a room from Helen and hadn't been told there would be a party. She was moving in a few days, as she didn't think her room was particularly desirable.

She let me worm out of her the new address and telephone number. When the long disputed and awaited taxi arrived that night, Mary Lona walked me outdoors and I kissed her. At that moment in the clinch, Helen turned on the porch light.

I went back to base and pretty much lost my social life until after I got my wings. Mary Lona moved into the new place and we didn't see each other for a time. Then as a new Flight Instructor at the base, I dug out her phone number. I proceeded to renew friendly visits with her.

I made my first date with Mary Lona to eat supper at Nixon's Cafe in downtown Corpus. She met me at the door of her new place and said she had a girlfriend who wanted a ride to town with us in the taxi I had waiting. She began to introduce us when I recognized the friend. I said we'd met already.

On our second date, I was waiting for Mary Lona to get ready when the unforgettable, beauteous and lovely Blanche Valley walked into the living room where I was seated. Mary Lona arrived shortly and began introductions. Blanche and I interrupted her to say we'd met before.

Our third date, I took Mary Lona to a night club for some dancing. The girl we called "Yankee" spoke to me on the dance floor.

Mary Lona moved again and began regaling me with tales of the antics of her landlady, a tall bossy woman with an eye for the men. This landlady was one of those large Texas characters in that land where everyone had to prove their manhood, including some women. In Mary Lona's stories I kept being reminded of the woman in town I knew as Maude Price. But Mary Lona and her landlady weren't living in the big house on a horse-shoe shaped drive. One evening I brought another Florida boy, Fred Register, to go out with Mary Lona's roommate Elsie Davis. Mary Lona began introducing me to her landlady, none other than Maude Price. For the fourth time I said, "Yes, we've met before."

Mary Lona was surprised. She said, "I have yet to introduce you to a woman you don't already know!"

I maintained she had managed to meet or introduce me to the only four women in town I knew.

She didn't believe me.

THOSE GOLDEN WINGS

Our operational phase of training was in seaplanes. They were designed for tasks in World War II that required multiple engines and a bigger size than carrier-based airplanes. When I landed a PBY or a PBM seaplane, I stalled out with the stern of my keel six inches above the water, in my pilot's compartment 50 feet above the water line.

My seaplane's wings jutting out from the top of the plane looked like giant ears flattened in the wind. Because it was a flying boat, it had aerodynamic lines and a boat keel's bottom. The PBY looked graceful in comparison to the PBM. But with the common seaplane design features, both planes were given impertinent names. Later on, in combat, the pilots we rescued thought the planes were as beautiful as angels; they still called us "Dumbos."

I found flying easier as I gained more skill and a feel for the seaplanes. I began to believe I would finish flight training, get those golden wings, and become an officer. Of course, I was also looking forward to higher pay and to flight pay, an additional 50 percent of base pay.

I made the May 26, 1943, graduating class. My orders read:
"Ensign Samuel A. Davis, A.V.N., U.S.N.R., 1315.
You will consider yourself detached from the
Naval Air Training Command, Corpus Christi,
Texas, at this date (26 May 1943). You will
proceed and report to the Naval Air Training
Command, NAS Corpus Christi, Tx., for duty
involving flying in a course of flight instructor
training and then to Basic Training at Cabanis
Field; you may delay ten (10) days in reporting."

Flight Instructor! I had got it right. I felt that of all the services
the Navy was the most prestigious. Within the Navy I believed the
pilots were the top dogs. Of the pilots, the instructors were the
cream of the crop. I had made it; I had earned those golden wings.

Mama came to Corpus to see me graduate, and we both caught
the train back to Florida. I was soon out on the East St. Andrew's
Bay with Uncle Mood again, catching speckled trout. We never
caught so many fish before or since.

Daddy and Mama were living in Panama City by then, in the
house where they would spend the rest of their lives. They settled
there on Mama's salary as a school teacher. The farm income was
gone. Daddy wouldn't take the government's payment for his land
because it didn't compensate for the free range cattle he had to
leave behind in the woods when they were moved off the homestead so fast.

Daddy sued the federal government, in wartime. Nothing was
yet determined in the suit.

Times had been hard before. The first month I had money from
a job had been December, 1936. I bought all our Christmas with
my first paycheck — a bag of oranges and a sack of pecans. We
were glad to have them! Now the times for my parents were that
hard again.

Daddy was never one to sit still. He opened up a trailer park on
the lawn adjacent to the house and eventually had to go to the bank
for a loan. He wore a hearing aid and thick glasses, and he walked
with a cane as a result of having been tossed around by a hurri-

cane-spawned tornado as a young man. He didn't let these infirmities stop him.

The banker was one of Mama's former pupils from Farmdale, come to town and making good. He and Daddy worked out terms, the amount to be borrowed, payments and interest. At the end of these arrangements the banker said, "Now, Mr. Pasco, what are you going to put up as collateral for this loan?"

"Collateral?" asked Daddy. "Yessir. You see, this is quite a bit of money, and we have to have something to back it up before we can lend you this much."

Daddy stared at him. He said quietly, "Son, if I can't get this loan on just my signature, I don't want your goddamned money."

Daddy stumped his cane on the floor and walked out.

At the door the banker caught up with him and agreed that his signature was enough for any man to trust. Daddy got the loan. It was the same way I got off the water as a naval aviator, how I earned my golden wings.

Daddy and I had pride in who we were, even if others didn't see it in us yet. He and I took risks we had to take, even when we had nothing left to risk with. Daddy had taught me to be determined, to adhere to my goal like pine tree gum. In May, 1943, I was ready for more adventure. I felt tough as a boiled owl.

COUSIN MARGIE

My first cousin Margie Kirkland wrote me from Florida. She had finished school and was working. She asked if I would like a visit from four young ladies — Valura Strauss, Juanita Gunn, her sister Rachel, and Margie. I wrote back yes, by all means.

I made reservations for them at the Nueces Hotel in Corpus and scurried around to find dates for them. They being naive little country girls, they wanted to be sure that I knew all of their escorts well. Trouble was, the people I knew well were other instructors who had been in town awhile and were pretty well booked up. Everyone I knew was awfully busy.

The first evening, I cajoled three of my friends to escort Margie and her friends, with me taking one of the Gunn girls. Margie and the girls came out to my quarters early, so I sent them to the Officer's Club to wait while I finished dressing. The bartender there asked the young ladies what they were having. Margie and the others didn't know one drink from another, so they asked for one of every drink on the bar list. It was Margie's introduction to "the hard stuff," and I wasn't told about it for 40 years. We had a lot of fun in town that evening.

The next night, I couldn't find a soul I knew to go with these young ladies. It so happened graduation was that day for a large class of cadets. These men had been in town only a few weeks and generally hadn't formed alliances in Corpus. As brand-new Ensigns they were running around everywhere getting ready to leave the next day.

Just before I headed upstairs at the Nueces Hotel to get the young ladies, I spied three brand new shiny wings and bars on Ensigns aimlessly walking about as if they were at a loss for what to do. I told them there were three dates for them upstairs, but the young ladies wouldn't go with anyone unless I knew them well. So if any of them asked, I was an old friend, had been for a long time — all of 4 minutes and 38 seconds. We had a barrel of fun.

It turned out that these young Ensigns were going to duty in Florida on the same train with Margie and her friends. I never told cousin Margie any different about my lengthy friendships with those fellows. I wondered if they kept up the fiction all the way to my home.

CADETS AND INSTRUCTORS

All the cadet pilots I instructed were divided into three kinds of students: hopeless cases; potentials; and the good ones. Some men were hopelessly inept at flying, even after they got by their elimination and primary training. You had to know where you and your plane were at all times. I could tell when I was sitting at ease in my pilot's seat that I was flying straight and level. To make a turn, I rolled one wing down and flew the plane unlevel. When I was again at ease in my seat in that position, I'd correctly balanced centrifugal force with any other force exerted on my aircraft. It was that kind of feel of the airplane that I'd try like the devil to get across to my students at the Corpus Christi Naval Air Station. But there would be a cadet every once in awhile who was unable mentally or physically to handle a plane; I would have to give up on him. I felt sorry for the "hopeless cases," not being able to fly.

Vito J. Gruzdis was one of the "potentials," men who had simply been mishandled before they got to me. His instructor was sick a good bit, and the flight officer asked me to fly Vito one day because he had gotten behind in flight training. Vito was on his eighth hop, supposedly ready for advanced training, and he couldn't stall the aircraft or land properly.

I put him through a couple of landings, and he was terrible. We flew over to a cove in the bay near Aransas Pass, north of Corpus, and set the plane down on the water. I told Gruzdis how it should be done, then told him we'd stay on that side of the bay and do landing after landing until he got it right. Then I took my hands and feet off the instructor's controls and said, "Vito, you've got it." Vito began to sweat. Two hours into the hop, Vito's shirt was sopping wet. We stopped on the water for another conference. I told him what he must do to get a passing "up-check" from me. If he did it, I'd write this up as an extra hop and recommend him to begin advanced training under the fabulous Fondren.

I'd been fortunate to take instructor training under Lt. Cdr. Fondren, an ex-Chief AP, enlisted pilot like George Toepher but with the rate of Chief. The Navy hadn't needed two years of college in a man to teach him to fly after all.

Fondren had thousands of hours in PBY seaplanes. He taught me to put the keel of the PBY six inches above the water just as it stalled out for a landing. He showed me how to land in rough water, hanging the aircraft's nose high on the prop when it stalled, so that a large wave wouldn't knock out the bow window where the bomb sight was mounted.

I always considered seaplanes to be trickier than other planes. Loving them didn't mean I was blind to their quirks. Fondren was one of the most skilled seaplane pilots I ever saw. Being recommended to him was a privilege worth going after.

Later in a bull session, I heard Vito tell his version of our day. "Sam wasn't my instructor, but he taught me more about flying in three hours of a two-hour hop than all the rest of the instructors I had. I've never worked that hard, before or since. He worked my butt off for an hour an a half, then he told me I had to take off and land, take off and land, all the way back in, then land at the base. I'd already used up all of Davis's penny pencils, so I tried to do the best I could, and found out I could do it!"

Lead pencils in those days could be bought for one cent apiece. These "penny pencils" happened to be slightly larger than the rivets used in the hull of the PBY. Sometimes landing too hard on the water sheared out some of the rivets, and water squirted up through the holes. I'd jam a penny pencil down the hole and break it off in there to keep the hull from leaking. We instructors carried a shirt full of penny pencils all the time. The squadron office bought them by the gross.Of course, the plane's rivets were replaced before its next flight.

The interior hulls of PBY seaplanes were open except for a catwalk in the center along the keel. The larger PBM seaplane interior hulls were closed by decking and gasoline tanks. The PBMs were so strong and rigid that we had no trouble with shearing rivets in them on hard landings. I always considered the PBM a much more rugged and solid seaplane than the PBY. Even among my beloved seaplanes, I had my favorites.

I met Harry Widener when we were cadets in Dallas. He was George Waller's nephew, and we used to gig flounder together. I had not seen or heard of him since I left Dallas.

I'd just found Harry through his wife Elsie, a legal secretary at Cabanis Field. When I met her, I told her I knew a guy named Harry Widener, and were they kin? She said, "That's my husband. He's instructing at Waldron Field."

Elsie was a real live wire. She was a native of Mobile and met Harry there when he played football for the University of Alabama against Spring Hill College. They were married after Harry got his wings, and he was assigned to Waldron Field, a new airfield just south of the main Corpus Christi Naval Air Station. He was instructing cadets in torpedo planes in a squadron named after the lost Torpedo Squadron 8, an earlier squadron led by Lt. Cdr. John Charles Waldron. Early in the battle of Midway, the entire squadron, all its planes and crews, were killed except for one pilot. It was a miracle that a PBY on patrol spotted the pilot, Ensign George Gay, after he floated in his life raft for 30 hours, and was able to rescue him. We all knew the story from *Life* magazine.

Harry and Elsie and I became best friends when we got together there in South Texas. They were home folks, and fun, and just what I needed to make liberty in Corpus a good time.

One day the Corpus Christi area had an especially vicious Blue Norther, the winter storms that sweep down unimpeded from

Canada to the coastal plains of Texas. For some reason, Harry and a student went flying anyway. They went into a flat spin and had to jump, but they were so low that their parachutes couldn't fully open before they hit the ground.

Both men were killed.

Harry was good at what he did, but he wasn't lucky. I escorted Elsie back home to Mobile on the train with Harry's body. I found six Ensigns at an operating ships' base in Mobile to supply Harry's military funeral as pall bearers. He deserved that, and it gave me something solid to do for Elsie.

Harry's sister Jewel Mashburn had been mother to him after his parents died; she was there. His Aunt Alma and Uncle George Waller and my Mama and Daddy also came to Mobile for the funeral. I was glad to see them all, but wished we could have been together for some other reason.

Harry's was the first death in war for me. Even going off to war, somehow we didn't think to be burying our friends in their teens and twenties. It was a terrible lesson, death out of time, that was being learned by millions of young people all over the world.

I was still hankering after the adventure of it all, but I knew after Harry's death that me and mine weren't too young to die either.

The next year, at night on the North Pacific, I was glad to have one of my old students, one of the good ones, on board with me. We were, thankfully, in a PBM. I was too busy to fool with penny pencils.

SEEING MARY LONA

My Officer's Club bill went so high that I had to figure out a better form of recreation. Fred Register had a fishing rod and gear, so I bought a rod and reel from a sailor. The two of us caught our own live bait in a small shrimp and minnow seine and waded into the bay to fish by some sea ramps that weren't being used to beach planes. Our aim was to save money and have the fun that fishing always brings me — eating fish.

One day late in the fall of 1943, I was practicing with a new fishing rod I had made from split bamboo. I didn't want to get wet, so I cast off from one of the float plane ramps in the lagoon, Laguna Madre. Something struck, got hooked, and I pulled it in. It was a beautiful fish with silver sides, grayish back, white underbelly, and a bright orange-colored patch beneath the throat. It grunted like all get out. I learned later that it was called the Golden Throated Croaker by South Texans.

I caught a couple of dozen of them and took them over to Mary Lona and her apartment mate Yvonne Wendell. I called her Wendell because that's how Mary Lona and the nurses addressed each other, by their surnames.

Wendell was a lovely, tall beauty from Rockport, Texas. Mary Lona was still "sort of" engaged to Army Sgt. Theodore Ressler, but I deliberately took the fish to her that day. She fried them to perfection. This, more than ever, let me know what a superb young lady she was. I figured that Ressler was a lucky guy. We gave all the other tenants in the building samples of our delicious fish.

Later, the owners, Mr. and Mrs. Taylor, took a notion to kick Mary

Lona and Wendell out of their apartment for some obscure reason. The other tenants, remembering the delicious fish, assured the Taylors that these were nice young ladies, and they would leave also if the Taylors made the nurses move. The Golden Throated Croaker was clearly the way to a lot of hearts that day.

When Mary Lona's brother Paul visited her, I took him up in my plane. It wasn't normal, and it may not have been legal, but it was done. I flew from Corpus out to Odem to the Forgy farm and showed it to Paul from the air. I knew the location of the farm well. The Odem Fan Marker, a radio beacon marking where the procedure turn was made on the let down leg of the Corpus Christi low frequency radio range station, was located 900 yards east of Mrs. Forgy's home.

If I was flying one of the airplanes when Mary Lona visited her mother at the farm, I serenaded her from the air. I dropped her a note tied around a corn stalk I had pulled up from the edge of one of the landing mats in the country. I often buzzed the farm house and waggled my wings at her when she ran out in the yard to see my plane.

During this time, Mary Lona nursed Mrs. Neiman, an elderly lady whose family owned about fifty apartments throughout Corpus. The family regularly came over to the hospital to visit their mother, and they talked freely about everything to Mary Lona. They often asked why she didn't marry one of those flyers at the base. She surreptitiously evaded all their questions and advice. Finally she told them she was dating one of the instructors in the big seaplanes on the bay. "Miss Forgy, you ought to marry that big man on the bay. You marry that big man on the bay, and we will rent you an apartment."

Given the tight housing shortage in Corpus during the War, this was a highly generous offer. They made it often to her.

Mary Lona would reply that the big man hadn't asked her to marry him. Then they would give her much advice. "You get him to see your figure. You invite him to your apartment for dinner and you purposely put the drinking glasses way up high on a shelf. You bend forward and reach up high, letting your dress pull up high above your knees. Then he will see your figure and he will get crazy. You marry that big man on the bay."

One day Mary Lona called me to say she and Wendell would be on the dock at the Cole Park doing some fishing. I had a flight with a couple of cadets on landing practice that morning, so we purposely did our landing along the bay front just off the dock. The cadets got a bit of pleasure seeing their instructor wave at his girlfriend on the dock. I felt as if I were indeed "the big man on the bay."

Mary Lona and I began to see more of each other. I wasn't looking for a wife, and she was spoken for by the Army sergeant.

MY LAST LOVE

Mary Lona was a native Texan, born in Sinton and raised on Rural Route 1 in Odem. When telephones finally came to that area, her family's number was assigned to Edroy, Texas. Mr. Forgy, her father, was originally named Monoah Davis, but he believed that his Uncle Monoah for whom he was named was a crook. By the time he was about ten years of age, he decided to change his name to Moral Dee. He had his teacher help him with the spelling, but the choice of "Moral" was his own. Everyone in his family accepted his decision, and probably for lack of a birth certificate, no court had to order his name changed. He was working as a carpenter in Missouri where he met and married Lona Frances Bozarth on March 21, 1911. That year, Mr. and Mrs. Forgy drove to what became the Forgy Farm. He bought 305 acres of rich black soil from a developer who had bought the whole area from the King Ranch. He took out a credit insurance policy on his mortgage that would later make all the difference to his widow and progeny. He was called "Dee" by everyone except his children, who called him "Papa." The legacy of his estate that Mary Lona valued most was "Papa's Bible."

Mary Lona's mother was called "Lona" by her peers, the matriarchs in the area. To her children she was "Mother." To all others, including me, she was "Mrs. Forgy." When I met her she was in her 50s, owner of high cotton farm land, chickens, and dairy cattle. The military was clothing millions in cotton, and eggs and butter were rationed. She always had all the gasoline she needed. Farm support payments saw them through the 1930s, and the credit insurance policy Dee had bought from the federal government paid off his mortgage on the farm when he died in 1937. Mrs. Forgy loved her husband and missed him all the rest of her life, but financial security and good health made this period the happiest time of her life.

As with me and my brothers, Mrs. Forgy's sons had been called to war. The oldest, Paul, was a classically trained violinist with a master's degree. Of course he was assigned to play the tuba with Army bands at Camp Beale in California for much of his service. Her youngest child was Ernest. He had a perforated ear-drum that kept him out of the military, so he took a job in a ship-building plant in California. He built the Liberty Ships that kept the war effort alive across two oceans. Mary Lona had her mother to herself for the duration.

The Forgy Farm is 33 miles outside of Corpus, far enough that Mary Lona had a life of her own but close enough to spend weekends on the farm as she chose. Soon I was invited out there for some weekends. Mrs. Forgy drove into Corpus to get Mary Lona and me. Arriving back at the farm, she parked the car at the front gate.

At bed time one visit, it was thought necessary to move the car to the garage for the night. I offered to move it, and Mary Lona went with me. She recalled later that we were "boodling;" she detested the words "making out." I remember that we had talked awhile when Mary Lona said, "You know, I don't know if I'll marry Ressler or not."

I thought to myself that if she "didn't know," then there must not be much of a binding force between them. I began to think that she would be an excellent wife. We continued to talk awhile in the car in the garage.

Suddenly I heard Mrs. Forgy outside. "Sister, are you children all right?"

"Yes, Mother."

I didn't know what to say, so I kept my mouth shut.

"Well, I was afraid you children might have been asphyxiated."

Mrs. Forgy turned and went up the drive to the house. Mary Lona and I went back into the house. I was hugely embarrassed. She thought it was funny. Later that same week I told Mary Lona I wanted her to think about me as a husband. Come Sadie Hawkins Day, I wanted an answer. Since Sadie Hawkins was a man-chasing character in Al Capp's "L'il Abner" comic strip, I couldn't tell whether she took this to be a country boy's joke or she thought about it being serious. After all, when her Mother was being funny she used words like "asphyxiated."

Mary Lona had never met a native Floridian. Even in those days we were a rarity, especially outside the state. I gave her a copy of Marjorie Kinnan Rawlings' book *The Yearling* and told her "These are my people."

For all that she was, a third generation Texan, and I a fourth generation Floridian, Mary Lona and I had many ideas and ways of living in common. Years later my Mama traced her Hallam genealogy for the DAR, and a distant cousin of Mary Lona's traced the Forgys back to the Norman French. Our immigrating ancestors were found in Middle Tennessee and Southern Kentucky in the 1800s, out from the Carolinas in the 1700s. We could then document our common heritage. After all, my Mama had taught me the meaning of "asphyxiated" too.

The Taylors finally got rid of Wendell and Mary Lona when they closed up their rooming house for repairs. Mary Lona prepared to move into a room in the home of Mrs. A. E. Riney on Caranchua Street. A very nice Southern lady from North Carolina, Mrs. Riney told me about her husband who had died a few years back. As a staff court reporter in the Army, he'd gone down into Mexico with Gen. John J. Pershing to ferret out the renowned bandit Pancho Villa. Mr. Riney must have loved the northern Mexico/South Texas area, as he declined an invitation from Henry Flagler to develop land in Florida and stayed in Texas instead. Had I heard anything about that man?

Well, yes. He'd become influential in Florida history. Henry Flagler opened up the lower east coast with the Florida East Coast Railway from Jacksonville to Miami. He developed St. Augustine, Flagler Beach, and railway stations throughout the state. He built the Flagler Hotel in Miami and constructed the final push of the Florida East Coast Railway on down the Keys, to the last one named Key West. I enjoyed bringing Mrs. Riney up to date on Mr. Flagler.

A night or two before the move from the Taylors to Mrs. Riney's,

Mary Lona and I were sitting on the front steps saying goodnight. I asked her would she marry me. She seemed to be dumbfounded with surprise, as she jumped up and ran to the top of the stair steps.

"Sam, this is serious business. I don't have an answer. Ask me again."

I didn't ask her again that night, but the discussions began between us. I was now one serious country boy.

One evening I came by and took her for a walk to Cole Park on the bay. The moon was up, and its light shimmering on Corpus Christi Bay was quite magical.

Mary Lona said, "Well, I guess we'll get married."

"You mean I got a chance in this here election?"

Always the country boy.

WAR TIME MARRIAGE

We went to Mrs. Forgy to tell her in an asking manner that we planned to get married on December 3, 1944. She said it was no surprise to her; she'd known it for a long time and had wondered when we would ever tell her.

From her decades of widowhood Mrs. Forgy told Mary Lona that whenever I asked her to go somewhere with me, she was to drop everything and go with her husband.

From her own marriage Mrs. Forgy gave us one piece of advice together: "Don't both of you get mad at the same time."

I've often wondered why we didn't always follow that.

On a weekend in the middle of November, 1944, Mary Lona and I visited her father's sister and brother-in-law, Aunt Alma and Uncle Bub Vickers in Sinton, about 14 miles from the farm. You could get there by way of Odem which is longer and a better road, or you could take the shorter route which winds through sandy land and was known as Poor Folks' Route. The black land of the Forgy Farm is highly productive and fertile. The sandy land being comparatively unproductive, it was characterized for many years by unkempt farm patches and small unpainted farm houses.

However, oil was found on the sandy land and not on the fertile farms. Within a generation, the financial relationships in the area switched top for bottom. By the 1940s, the small houses were still unpainted, but there was an oil well or two pumping in the back yards. The remaining farmers still called it Poor Folks' Route.

The phone rang while we were at Aunt Alma's, and she came back into the room to say it was for me. This was most amazing. It was Homer Reed, my friend and fellow instructor, calling to say that several of us instructing in seaplanes were called now to overseas duty and would need to pick up our orders Monday morning. Reed had called Odem because he knew I was visiting my fiancee there. The operator was a friend of the Forgys who knew they had no phone, so she put the call through to Sinton for him to leave a message with the Vickers. I just happened to be there.

Wedding plans went on hold until I could read my orders. On Monday I found they were:

> "On or about December 1, 1944, you will consider
> yourself detached from the Naval Air Training
> Command, Corpus Christi, Texas, and report for
> duty involving flying to the Operational Training
> Unit Four (OTU-4) to train in PBM aircraft for
> further duty in the forward area of the North
> Pacific for duty in search and rescue operations.
> You may delay 10 days in reporting."

I saw Mary Lona before she went on duty at 11 p.m. Monday. We would still get married on December 3, go to New Orleans by Greyhound bus for our honeymoon, return by December 10, and check into OTU-4.

Our wedding was held after the Sunday evening service at the First Baptist Church in downtown Corpus. I suspected that Mary Lona wanted her friends and cousins to attend at least one Southern Baptist service in their lives. That night, the pastor, Dr. Cawker, announced there would be a wedding directly after the service for which all were invited to stay if they so desired. He also joked that he had tried to advise the groom against it, but I just would not listen. Most of the congregation stayed.

Mrs. Forgy was Matron of Honor, as Mary Lona had an embarrassment of riches in close women friends and didn't want to choose just one among them. Blanche Valley, Yvonne Wendell and Elsie Davis (no kin to me) were her bridesmaids. I had Homer Reed as my Best Man and Bob Hammer and Jim Lunt as groomsmen, all Naval aviators.

Sid Rigell from Panama City and another aviation radioman lit the candles. Mary Lona was escorted down the aisle by Uncle Bub, the closest male relative of her father's generation. My parents came to the wedding on the bus from Florida, beginning a life-long affection with my mother-in-law on this visit. All our collection of brothers were on war duty elsewhere.

Mary Lona had taken her Mother and me along to pick out her wedding dress. In the stillness of formal black and white pictures, she looked elegant and chaste in its silk satin. Our daughter wore this dress 28 years later in her own wedding. In living color and in motion, the dress took on a demure sensuality that is certainly appealing to a bridegroom. My son-in-law said it was obvious I helped pick it out in 1944.

In New Orleans, Mary Lona and I stayed at the Hotel Monteleone and walked Canal Street in the honeymooner's fog that was more gripping for the news of what lay ahead for us. We had wanted to honeymoon in Mexico, but by December, 1944, military personnel were not allowed to spend the night there. We bought a serape for my Mama as a kind of token of trips we would later take, but not while there was a war on. I really wanted to live through this, come back home, and see Mexico with Mary Lona someday. I suspected there was more than one kind of life-time adventure available to me now.

Back in Corpus, Mary Lona packed away her wedding gifts in anticipation of the peripatetic life of a Navy wife.

She didn't pack up just yet the sterling silverware her Mother had given us as a wedding present. It was a pattern with a figure like a pine cone on the handles, reminiscent of native Florida.

Mary Lona had read all of the Marjorie Kinnan Rawlings books by then. Mrs. Neiman and her family were true to their promise to Mary Lona. We lived in one of their apartments for a few weeks, then they moved us into an apartment in her home.

The family was charming in their gratitude to Mary Lona for having nursed their matriarch back to health. We had six months together in Corpus and in San Diego before I shipped out. We didn't know if these were the only months we would ever have. We couldn't know that we were with men and women who would be closer to us than brothers and sisters, all the rest of our lives.

CREW 5 OF THE WILLIE-7

We called Don Flaherty from Cincinnati, Ohio, "Irish" because he deserved it. He must have kissed the Blarney Stone, as he made our war seem like a merry thing. He especially told on me about the first muster of the crew I carried into combat:

"I'll never forget the first time I saw Sam. There I was in Corpus Christi, Texas, a Southern town with a good Catholic name. Sheila and the baby were with me over in North Beach in a room they called an apartment. It was the morning of our first muster as Crew 5. I'm standing out there on the concrete, looking over these other guys, and they start calling out our names. Pretty soon everyone's answered, but I keep hearing, 'Lt. jg Samuel A. Davis.' No answer. Finally, Sam answers, and there he is with fishing gear all over him, beating up on a gar. I think to myself, this is the man who's going to see whether I come back from the war? Blessed Mary, Joseph, and all the saints preserve us!"

To someone from a river city I must have been a sight, emerging from the water after gigging flounder all night. But I never could leave good eating on the bottom of a shallow bay.

I was most fortunate to have Tuck Dicken at that first muster, too. His real name was "Carl Mervin," and he was a native of Kentucky, so we called him "Tuck." He said I taught him how to fly. I was instructing in PBYs in Corpus when Tuck was assigned to me the first time. He told me he was ready to wash out, that he had one last chance.

I told Tuck, "If you know what you have to do, let's go up."

We went out and back on a morning hop. After lunch, we passed through the ready room, and I picked up the funny papers. It was Sunday. They were in color. I never could resist them.

When we got out to the plane, I told him to take off, fly across the Corpus Christi Bay, and shoot landings where we'd been that morning. Then I took my feet off the rudder. I picked up the funnies with both hands, so they weren't on the wheel. I proceeded to read the funny papers, so my eyes were elsewhere.

Tuck had in one morning gone from a "potential" to one of the good ones. I didn't act this confident with every cadet I instructed.

I found out later that Tuck's reaction was just what I wanted and expected from him. He said to himself, "By golly, this guy has a lot of confidence in me."

When we got back on the ground, I told Tuck, "You can fly."

Tuck replied, "Yeah! I can do it!"

From Corpus, Tuck had gone to Banana River, Florida, for more seaplane experience. I sure was glad to see him back in Corpus again. He was an old country boy, just like me.

Crew 5 was formed as part of the push into the North Pacific. We were mobilizing to invade Japan, our biggest response yet to the bombing of Pearl Harbor, Guam, and Manila. We were going to fly Air-Sea Rescue in PBM-5s, the fifth modification of the Martin PBM "Mariner" seaplane. The plane carried 11 of us and any pilots we rescued, replete with battle stations, bunks, and a fully functioning galley.

PBMs were slower than fighter planes, but no fighter pilot had enough room to get up and go down the ladder to cook a steak or brew a fresh pot of coffee in the galley.

We formed up in Crew 5 in Corpus. There we were actually Crew number 5 in the squadron. The seaplane first assigned to us as a crew was a PBM-5, Bureau #59227, with the side number W-7, hence the "Willie-7." Planes and squadron crew numbers changed, but we called ourselves "Crew 5 of the Willie-7" everywhere we went, and we knew who we were.

BROTHERLY LOVE

My first trip outside the United States was a navigation training flight to Coco Solo, Panama. All of us in Crew 5 anticipated the adventure avidly, especially me and Second Radioman Raleigh Slawson. He had already flown seaplanes in the Caribbean Sea, patrolling for German submarines to keep the Panama Canal open for the Allies. Slawson looked forward to being almost a tourist down there.

We were due to return to home base after one night in Coco Solo, but when it was time to leave, we couldn't get the engines started. We tried and tried. Honest.

Panama base maintenance couldn't find out why the engines wouldn't start. Few maintenance people in 1945 knew about the electric choke on the new engines of the PBM-5 we flew. When Panama base maintenance finally got the engines started for us, it was too dark for us to take off for Corpus.

That night, the two co-pilots, Tuck and Richard "Dixie" Runstrom, and I bought a magnanimously large stalk of bananas from a street vendor. We hung them in the galley in the bow of the seaplane.

The next morning the engine problem mysteriously cleared up, and we headed back to Corpus. About two hours into the flight, Tuck asked the crew to bring the bananas up to the flight deck. We learned Yes, there were no bananas. However, the crew told us that they had enjoyed them immensely.

Panama wasn't on the rationing that we had back in the States. The hams we bought at the Army commissary in Coco Solo didn't suffer the same fate as the bananas. They rode home safely in the "dog house," a housing on the top of the PBM built for the radar antennae. Aerodynamics dictated a housing with room left over that was just right for the storage of meat beyond the limits of our red stamps. You could say we were smuggling, if the statute of limitations has run out.

While we waited for clearance to take off, Harry "Brownie" Brown, our plane captain and chief engineer, allowed as how he "probably" flooded the engines the day before with the electric choke. Then of course he "remembered" how to fix the problem that very morning. Fancy that!

Two hours after we lifted off, Corpus Christi Control told us that weather had closed them in. I asked for a diversion to Key West Naval Air Station. We had enough of Panama tourism in two days. I figured I could talk Control into the navigational training and the experience we could get in the diversion.

I really wanted a chance to see my brother Carl, a Coast Guard mechanic and machinist, a "Motor Mac." He was stationed in Fort Lauderdale. The crew were amenable to seeing Key West after I described it to them.

Control diverted us, and I had a chance to catch up with Carl in Key West before I had to leave for Corpus. I was awfully glad to see him on shore duty. He was back from running Coast Guard landing boats in the Allied invasions of North Africa, Sicily, and Italy, going time after time up on beaches that became famous for their slaughter.

I got him on the phone. "Nick! It's me. Hop a plane on over here to Key West. I'm here for a couple of days. We can catch some fish."

"Why, Sambo. Good to hear your voice. I'll be right over, but I'm going to catch the bus."

"A bus? That'll take more time. I've got to go back to Corpus when the weather clears over there. Listen, you'll take hours on the bus. You can get on the mail plane and be over here for the next tide."

"Well now, Sam, I don't have a hankering to be on an airplane anyway. They're dangerous. I'll be on the next bus; meet me at the

Greyhound station." That was a heck of a note — Carl had made all those landings under heavy fire in light landing craft on all those bloody beaches, but he wouldn't fly the width of Florida for the risk.

Every rare once in awhile, Carl acted like an older brother. Even using "Nick," our childhood name for each other, I couldn't persuade him to fly.

THE LIVING
BOAT HOOK

C rew 5 developed a rescue strategy that I think was unique. Irish and Carroll "Willie" Wilson, Second Gunner from Oxford, North Carolina, were assigned to the bow. Willie threw out the life preservers to the survivors. Irish moored the buoys. It was how they did it.

Slawson always said, "Back then Irish wasn't as big as a nickel bar of soap after a wash."

We took great pride in how fast we could pull a survivor aboard and get ready for take-off. Willie could throw passes real well — he'd played football in college. We'd land in the water and taxi over to the pilots in their life rafts. Willie threw out the life preserver ring with a line attached.

When the survivor grasped the ring, the crew pulled in the line. When they'd pulled him close enough, Irish hung onto the sill of the after station door, and the crew gripped each other's forearms to make a chain strong enough to hold a scared pilot. They grasped him by the arms and vigorously helped him clamber aboard. But if Willie needed a bit more extension to reach a survivor or a buoy, he held Irish out the bow door of the plane. The crew held Irish's feet up off the deck. Irish reached out as far as he had to get the job done. I swear, Willie extended Irish just like a boat hook. I never saw anything like it, before or since.

factors conducive to causing a longer run before breaking suction with the water and getting airborne. It took such a long takeoff that we couldn't do the regular pattern of flying out over Point Loma. Instead we curved around and flew over the ship channel pass to the ocean. I remember that Mary Lona, Sheila Flaherty, Evelyn Dicken, and Ruth Brown were on the dock watching our takeoff and waving feverishly.

That evening our wives dried the tears they would not let us see. Mary Lona and Evelyn parted company at the bus station, going south and north to their childhood homes. It was sad.

I left a heart full of love with Mary Lona, standing on that dock waving at my airplane as she'd done so many times before. I left a nation mourning President Roosevelt's death on April 12, 1945, the man who led us out of hard times and within reach of military victory. But I thought of none of this. My mind was on war, the highest adventure a young man could know.

Mary Lona Forgy, beautiful nurse

Samuel Adams Davis, Naval Aviator

L to r: Harry (Brownie) Brown, C.W. (Willie) Wilson,
and Don (Irish) Flaherty, the living boat hook

Cousin Margie visiting Sam on base

*Above left: Sam flies PBY to impress Mary Lona, Above right: Mary
Lona points Sam out; Below left:Mary Lona and Sam at Forgy farm
Below right: Evelyn and Tuck Dicken, Mary Lona and Sam, fishing*

Sam and Mary Lona

GOODBYE

In late April, 1945, Crew 5 left Corpus Christi Naval Air Station by car, train, bus, and airplane for the Naval Air Station at San Diego, California.

San Diego was like a second honeymoon trip for Mary Lona and me. We rode horses in the California hills with Tuck and his wife Evelyn, Dixie and his date. We had ridden horses throughout our childhoods, so rented mounts were no big deal. Later when I was overseas, Mary Lona sent me a bound booklet of the photographs of all of us that day. She always looked good to me, but especially the day I got those pictures.

Mary Lona and I often went down to Mission Beach with the rest of Crew 5, wives, sisters, cousins, and girlfriends. The first trip we waited for the bus we were told to take, the "La Hoya." Too much time passed and too many buses went by without being ours. Finally we asked a Californian when the La Hoya bus was coming. He told us several La Hoya buses had stopped for us already and we hadn't boarded them. Come to find out, we were to get on the next bus marked "La Jolla." What a goof! It was these kinds of laughs that kept us from dwelling on how short our time together might turn out to be.

The time came fast on us to be ready for the transpac flight to Kaneohe in Hawaii. We put in a bomb-bay tank to have ample fuel for the 2,000 mile flight. The vast Pacific was always a factor in our part of the war. This first flight would get us about halfway to our war-zone, going over water the whole way. We were going to get a taste of the immensity from which we would be expected to pluck our brothers in arms and bring them out to safety. But first we had to take off. We were heavily loaded, the water at the far end of the bay was dead calm, and no wind was there to help — all factors conducive to causing a longer run before breaking suction with the water and getting airborne. It took such a long takeoff that we couldn't do the regular pattern of flying out over Point Loma. Instead we curved around and flew over the ship channel pass to the ocean. I remember that Mary Lona, Sheila Flaherty, Evelyn Dicken, and Ruth Brown were on the dock watching our takeoff and waving feverishly.

That evening our wives dried the tears they would not let us see. Mary Lona and Evelyn parted company at the bus station, going south and north to their childhood homes. It was sad.

I left a heart full of love with Mary Lona, standing on that dock

LOSS AND REPLACEMENT

While we were in Hawaii, our Second Engineer, John Reid, contracted a bad case of athlete's foot and had to go to sick bay for treatment. Reid came from Tulsa, Oklahoma, and was the one USN Regular among the rest of us Reservists in Crew 5. On the morning we left Hawaii, a hospital spokesman said that Reid couldn't be released by then. When he could be released, they'd send him out to us.

On July 10, 1945, without Reid, Crew 5 readied a brand new quarter-of-a-million-dollar PBM-5 to fly to Saipan to deliver as a replacement to a squadron there. We spent the night at Johnston Island, hardly bigger than its runway, with an elevation about 18 inches above sea level. I was glad to have the whole lagoon to land in. We spent the next night at Kwajalein in the Marshall Islands, and lost a day on my first crossing of the International Date Line. On 13 July, we delivered the seaplane to Saipan and reported to the Senior Officer Present (SOP) for transport to Okinawa. We had flown 3,500 miles from Hawaii and still not reached our destination for duty. A man could get lost in all that expanse.

In three more days, the SOP gave us another PBM-5 to take to a squadron, not ours, on Okinawa. On July 16th, we departed under orders for Kerama Retto some 30 miles southwest of Okinawa. Within three hours of Kerama Retto, we received a message to go to Chimu Wan, a bay about halfway down the east coast of Okinawa.

We were Air-Sea Rescue for all the forces — Army, Navy, and Marines. Our forces had taken parts of Okinawa and some small islands to the south. The southern end of Okinawa was secured by the time we got there, but U.S. Marines still fought in the hills. The Navy surface fleet was harbored in Buckner Bay on the southeast coast of Okinawa. The seaplane force was in Chimu Wan, just to the north of Buckner and separated from it by only a few rocks and coral heads jutting above the water.

We had no charts or radio aid location of our new destination. I remembered how ducks and geese land on a pond. Ducks will land where other ducks are, and geese do the same. I had a reputation for patience (undeserved) because as a boy I spent hours waiting for spooked ducks and geese to return to a shore of St. Andrew's Bay, to shoot down a good dinner. Taking a cue from their landing behavior, I looked for other PBMs. When we saw some, we landed beside them. It was a crazy way to treat a quarter of a million dollars. After we landed for the night and went aboard our ship, a seaplane tender, I carried the analogy further. We, the ship and the planes, were sitting ducks for enemy planes.

The next day, our squadron moved from Kerama Retto to Chimu Wan and caught up with us. We finally arrived at our front of World War II when we went aboard the USS Pine Island, one of the largest seaplane tenders in that area. It had to be: it housed our squadron — VH-3, a fleet maintenance unit, and the Task Force Commander for Air-Sea-Rescue in the North Pacific.

VH-3 was and is an official Navy entity: "V" for heavier-than-air craft, "H" for hospital. It had been commissioned for about a year when we went out to replace a war-weary crew. At that time, VH-3 had nine crews and six seaplanes. No one crew ever had a plane to call their own, but we called ourselves "Crew 5 of the Willie-7" every chance we had.

Then we got word that Reid's story wasn't going to have a happy ending. He had diabetes and would get a medical discharge. Any one of us would have been shaken up by the diagnosis, but Reid was the one with a dream of a 30-year Navy career.

Reid wrote us a cheery letter from Oklahoma saying he felt like a "lucky 4-F," a man who could legally be at home during the War because of a medical condition that exempted him from the Draft. But his wife Louise told us, "It nearly killed Johnny. He said he'd rather they cut off both his legs than discharge him from the Navy." It was a hell of a thing to be left behind.

Reid's replacement was Ray Lutz, from Olmstead Falls, Ohio. His name meant nothing to me, but when he arrived I remembered meeting him in Hawaii. Tuck and I had been hitchhiking along the side of the road. Lutz was headed back to quarters in a weapons carrier and picked us up. We inevitably started talking about the planes.

Lutz complained about all these ex-PBY pilots swaggering on board a PBM, believing they could just up and fly them. He said, "I know from the engineering that the two planes have different flight characteristics, but what can I do about it? I don't have a crew assignment. I'm assigned to HedRon (headquarters at Kaneohe), painting equipment."

Tuck and I didn't tell Lutz we were two former PBY pilots flying PBMs.

Lutz told us later about his joining Crew 5, "Finally, I pulled an assignment with a PBM crew already at the forward area around Okinawa. I flew out with Vito Gruzdis and asked him if he knew my new PPC, Samuel A. Davis. I hadn't remembered Sam's and Tuck's names, they were just two guys I'd picked up hitchhiking. Gruzdis told me everybody wanted to fly with Sam Davis; he kept a cool head, never letting things bother him. You couldn't get lost flying with Sam.

"When I got out there, the crew greeted me and said their pilots were forward. I walked on up to meet my new officers, Tuck and Sam, two ex-PBY pilots now flying this PBM.

"I wanted a wave to come up and knock me over the side, right there."

So Lutz joined us in Okinawa. I teased him about his opinion of us pilots. He was right — I'd already had to experiment with where the PBM's nose should be on takeoff because I didn't feel the way I'd done it in PBYs was getting it exactly right in the PBM yet.

I was glad to have Lutz with his experience, but I hated what happened to Reid.

AT THE FRONT

On July 18, 1945, we rescued some pilots without taking them aboard. It was our first combat hop; we met with the Patrol Plane Commander (PPC) of the crew we were relieving. He stayed over from his tour of duty in the forward area to fly with us on our first mission. The rest of his crew had already shoved off to home, rest, relocation and shore duty. On this trip, he gave us pointers on what to expect and do.

We flew to the southern tip of Kyushu, itself the southernmost of the four large islands of the Japanese homeland, and found four men in a life raft about seven miles offshore. We came in low to survey the sea for landing, finding the swells so close together and rough that an open sea landing beside them would be too hazardous to attempt. The other PPC said, "Just my luck! I won't bust up a plane on my last trip — let's do something else."

We dropped a couple of long-life smoke lights by the fellows in the rubber raft and headed north to Kagoshima Bay about 10 miles away. The other PPC said we'd land there and taxi out to rescue the four pilots. We circled above the shoreline inside this small, round, calm bay on the south tip of Kyushu, and squared away for a landing into the wind coming through the pass to the ocean.

As we were touching down in the water but not slow enough to be settled in it, a large ocean swell swept into the bay. It hit us head on and bounced us into the air without enough airspeed to keep us airborne. My hand was already on the throttles and the prop pitch, and I two-blocked them (a Navy term from sailing days for pushing something as far as it will go). The other PPC hit my hand with his, trying to send them further than I had, almost breaking my hand in his desire not to lose the plane in Kagoshima Bay.

We picked up airspeed by inches. We didn't have quite enough airspeed to climb, but we had enough that we wouldn't stall either. We were mushing — dropping down in a sloppy, sickening, soft kind of way. If we couldn't stop mushing back into the bay, the seaplane would eventually crack up when we hit the water. I'd seen a seaplane pilot die in San Diego Bay when he mushed; his plane just seemed to explode on impact.

That day we made it into the air. We climbed out, flew back to the survivors in the life raft, and called the nearest surface ship, a destroyer escort about 40 miles away. Being in the air, we could radio further than someone on the water. And in those days, the men weren't equipped with radios in their life rafts. As we circled over their raft that day, we sent the Morse Code letters "M," two dashes, and "O," three dashes. This gave a humming sound for the ship to take bearings on us as it headed our way. We flew low over the survivors to see if they were in good shape. They were. They'd last long enough for us to get other help to them.

We flew over the survivors and dragged a line with a float-worthy package attached to the end of the line. They were drifting in the wind, so our drop point to reach them was downwind. That way they would drift into the package. We dipped the plane so that the line touched the water within their reach. The first package was a note telling them a ship would be there in about three hours.

We continued to circle above the survivors in their raft. When the ship was within five miles, we maneuvered again to drop a couple of long-lasting smoke lights beside the raft. Of course, by then our gas supply was running low. When we were sure the surface ship had sighted them, we headed back to Okinawa. In about 30 minutes, the ship radioed that it had picked them up and all were in good shape. We were credited with effecting the rescue without having to land and take off in the swells of the open sea.

When the other PPC left us the next morning, we thanked him for showing us how to do the work. He thanked us for our luck to survive his last — and our first — flight to Japan.

Our second mission was July 23rd, a trip into the ocean to the location where a patrol plane reported they thought they had sunk a Japanese submarine. We were to look at debris and oil slicks to identify whether they were from a submarine. I had no sympathy for Japanese warriors, but I sure hated the thought of anyone dying at sea, especially in a sunk submarine all cooped up with nothing but seawater for air. Keep me aloft, thank you.

The Operations Officer of VH-3, Lt. Cdr. R. P. "Muddy" Waters, and our squadron Commander, Lt. Cdr. William D. Bonvillian, told us that the Wing Commander wanted us to land and pick up some debris for positive identification. To me, the Wing Commander sounded like someone who hadn't almost mushed back into the waters of a small Japanese bay. Bonvillian, on the other hand, had taxied a damaged PBM back to base rather than risk his crew and survivors by attempting a hazardous open sea takeoff. Waters and Bonvillian told us they didn't want to risk losing a plane and a crew unless a man's life was at stake. That far out from land, the ocean was too rough for a safe landing. They sounded to me like people who knew what we were up against out there.

We went to the location of the report, about 90 miles east of Amami O Shima, found nothing, and set up a square ladder search. This was our normal pattern of flying a grid, back and forth, turning at 90 degree angles and criss-crossing to cover an area of ocean thoroughly. We found nothing in the search area. A thunder squall came over the area, so we flew 30 miles south to clear weather. There we found the debris where it ought not to be. From the air, an oil slick and debris appeared to be from a sunken submarine. The squall blew over toward us again, roughening up the ocean, so we went back to base without landing.

We had flown two missions and didn't make an open sea landing and takeoff. Lutz had joined us July 24th for his first trip with us. The next day would bring our third mission of the war. It started out routinely enough.

ON CALL

July 25, 1945, Crew 5 of the Willie-7 took off from Chimu Wan about 10:00 a.m. for a routine flight to Adm. William "Bull" Halsey's Third Fleet Carrier Task Forces steaming 300 miles off the shore of Japan.

Our forces had been sneaking up into Japan, making bombing and strafing raids on the enemy's mainland for three or four days, then pulling back to safety for a few days. Shortly before the morning of July 25th, our forces began to raid Japan around the clock. I flew the seaplane over the Fleet, amazed to see the vast strike forces in the four Carrier Task Groups. I was stunned with a sense of the enormity of what the Navy could do to Japan with what we had amassed. After circling for an hour or so, the crew and I received a message from Group Commander saying that two pilots had gone down in the Inland Sea of Japan near the Japanese Kure Naval Base. The message was:

"We have definitely one and possibly two targets 25 miles southeast of Kure. We want to try a rescue. It is a dangerous mission. Group Commander is not ordering you to go; you may volunteer at your own discretion."

There was a waiting silence while I thought to myself, "Trust in luck. No, trust in God." I keyed the mike and said, "We'll go."

Group Commander came back on the air, "You may head for the coast of Japan."

We turned the Willie 7 to the west.

They continued:

"We have no fighter escort available for you now. We will try to get fighters back in, gassed, armed and ready to send to you for cover. If we

do not have fighter cover for you by the time
you reach the coast, then you may turn back,
for your safety would be in jeopardy inside Japan
alone."

I breathed a prayer as we headed to the coast of Japan. "Almighty, powerful and loving God, save the crew, the plane, and me."

INSIDE JAPAN

W e flew out from the Third Fleet toward the coast of Kyushu and Shikoku, two of the largest four is lands of the Japanese homeland. We were headed to Bungo Suido, a strait that leads to the Inland Sea between Shikoku and the northern tip of Kyushu, the southernmost island of Japan. Group Commander sent sporadic encouraging messages, but no fighter escorts. The day before, Lt. jg J. R. "Spider" McGill and his crew had plucked a survivor from Kobe Bay. They'd had an escort of 16 fighters and been attacked by air, shore batteries, and ships. They picked up a survivor within sight of pedestrians on the streets of Kobe, and made it back.

When we were about 70 miles from the coast of Japan, we heard from Lt. Warren Smith, leader of a sortie of four F6F "Hellcat" fighters from the carrier USS Bonhomme Richard. He said, "We have enough fuel to take the Dumbo in, and I can stay with him three or four hours. We'll be over Slippery Sal in 40 minutes."

Not 16 fighters. Four. It was certainly better than nothing. The PBMs we flew in VH-3 had been stripped of nonessential items and armor plate to increase our range. We still had three gun turrets, each with two .50 calibre machine guns, at the tail, the top, and the bow. We could fire in almost any direction; we just had to be careful not to fire into the wing floats.

There had been two more .50 calibre guns, on hydraulic mounts on each side of the after-station. VH-3 routinely removed these to get rid of excess weight and to let us pull in survivors quicker through the doors in the waist of the plane. We compensated for our reduced weapons by having fighter escorts on our rescue missions.

We were still vulnerable, especially when we landed in the water and took survivors aboard. Then we concentrated on pulling them in, cocking back into the wind, and getting into the air safely with all aboard. Winds, waves, and swells were treacherous, but enemy fire was a deadly hazard. I was glad to hear from Warren Smith and his buddies, though they were only four.

We would meet up with them at Slippery Sal, a rendezvous point for our planes over the ocean, about 20 miles southeast of the entrance to Bungo Suido Strait. The "L" and "R" sounds in the name were almost impossible for a native Japanese speaker to pronounce correctly. Native English speakers could pronounce it repeatedly with every "R" and "L" in place. If the Japanese found out about the rendezvous and tried to lure any of us there for an ambush, they couldn't fool us when "Slippery Sal" was pronounced "Srippery" or "Slippelly" or "Srippelly Saru."

At Slippery Sal, we stationed two fighters on each side and a little ahead of us. All of us went down to 150 feet to be below radar cover. We observed radio silence except for short-range VHF interplane communication. No need to let a diligent Japanese radio operator get a fix on us from our chatter.

All five planes headed up Bungo Suido. We passed by a small island in the middle of the Strait with a light tower and a house on it, and not much room for anything else. There was a strong possibility of a gun emplacement there, but we had no weapons fire from it the morning of July 25th. Further along we passed the tip of a narrow peninsula, jutting way out into Bungo Suido, with a lighthouse tower on it. We cut by this tower without difficulty. Just beyond the peninsula we were inside the Inland Sea and headed toward the reported position of our survivor.

Just inside the Inland Sea near the shoreline, we heard the two fighters on our starboard side: "Look at those two planes. They look like trainers."

"They must've borrowed a couple of N3Ns from us."

"Red Leader 2 to Red Leader 1, permission to make a kill."

We knew by then that Kamikaze suicide pilots trained in this area. They needed to learn to fly for their final missions of plowing into our ships and island bases. In our forward area, since April, 1945, Allied forces had already suffered massive losses of life and equipment to Kamikaze attackers, some of them in planes that looked like trainers. If we had been headed out rather than in, our fighter escort would have fired to take them out of action. But Warren Smith replied, "Red Leader 1 to Red Leader 2. No. They're no threat to us. Let's lead the Dumbo in."

FINDING YODER

B y mid-afternoon, we reached the reported position of the survivors and had no sighting of them. So we turned into a direction with the wind and flew for five minutes. Still no sighting. It always took some time to get out to where the survivors of a ditched plane were reported to be. Meanwhile, winds and ocean currents would take them out of that position. We wanted to get to them before they drifted into sight of enemy ships and planes or onto the shores of Japan. We set up the normal ladder search pattern.

In our search, we began to draw fire on the leg of the pattern that took us near the shore. We saw the smoke of Japanese guns firing at us from the hills along the shoreline. The gun batteries were trying to get our range. I comforted myself with the notion they didn't seem to be anti-aircraft guns. My plane could fly faster than most shore batteries could track us.

We continued to see the puffs of gunfire headed in our direction, but we stuck to our search. Suddenly we were rewarded with the sight of bright yellow-green dye marker in the water, readily visible. We recognized we had passed over this survivor once and by him twice. He'd been relying on shooting signals with his small verys pistol. We hadn't seen the flares from his pistol in the bright sunlight.

In all this time, our survivor drifted within range of those shore batteries. That was where we would have to land to reach him. We set the plane down quickly in smooth waters, pulled him aboard, and closed the after-station doors, all in about five minutes. We wanted to get done and get out of there!

While we took on this survivor, the plane cocked 30 degrees out of the wind direction. I would have to turn into the wind before we could finally lift off the water and get outside the range of the Japanese guns.

A seaplane hull is built in two sections. The first section runs from the bow to amidships, then, after a vertical step up of about eight inches, the hull continues to the tail. This innovation in design allowed all seaplanes to break the suction of the water. Upon takeoff, the front section of the hull lifts out of the water first, making the craft more maneuverable. At this point, the after section is still on the water. Without the step, seaplanes wouldn't lift reliably into the air, especially coming off smooth water. I could turn the Willie-7 into the wind quicker if I turned after we "planed up on the step."

We began the takeoff run from the Inland Sea while still 30 degrees to the left of the wind line because that happened to be the direction the plane was pointed when the after-station reported "Ready for takeoff." When we started the takeoff run, we stayed on this heading until the plane was on the step, then we turned into the wind. Out of the port window I noticed a dozen geysers in the water from the Japanese guns firing on us. We had been on the water long enough for them to get our range. Their shells hit at the place we would have been had we not turned.

Red Leader 1, Warren Smith, radioed his praise for us that we saw the Japanese fire and turned out of the way to miss it. He affirmed that if we'd proceeded as we were first headed we would have been hit. A dozen shells would have finished us off.

I thought at the time that we'd passed through the worst danger we would face out there. I was wrong.

We had picked up Ensign Calvin B. "Bert" Yoder, a Hoosier from Kokomo, Indiana. He'd been flying a Hellcat F6F from the USS

Randolph. Before we reached him he drifted in the water over four hours toward the Japanese shore. Twice when Japanese surface ships came near him, he had slipped over the off-side and hung onto the raft underwater. Apparently his ruse to make his raft seem empty worked, and no Japanese seaman decided to use the raft for target practice that day.

Yoder figured that at night he would paddle ashore and try to hide out. Stories circulated in the forward area about pilots who found the Allied underground in China and reached home through Asia or the Soviet Union. It was more likely he would be detected as an alien in Japan and sent to the torture of a Japanese prison camp. There was just so much damned luck about surviving that way.

Yoder had no idea he would be rescued so far inside Japanese waters. Pilots like Yoder flew their missions with unspoken dread. They saw their bombing and strafing assignments as one-way streets. As had the other pilots, Yoder had inflicted significant damage to the enemy anyway, crippling a Japanese destroyer before he ditched.

We asked him what he was thinking about out there. He said, "Home. I was thinking about home. I was thinking Kokomo was a long way off."

I thought Yoder threw me a kiss as I coasted by on the landing to pick him up. The crew said he kissed the deck of the PBM when they pulled him aboard. When he got to the flight deck, he told me with a big grin, "MIGHTY glad to be aboard, sir."

Years later I got an inkling as to Yoder's behavior from an Army Air Corps pilot who had been shot down over Berlin and spent a year and a half in a German POW camp. We were swapping flight stories in the bright, happy dining room of an Officer's Club when he spoke of how grateful the rescued pilots must have been for the Dumbos. He kept trying to tell me something. Then he began to weep.

INSIDE JAPAN
ALONE

A Japanese submarine had been detected in the water close to Yoder, and there were a few Japanese surface craft not far from the area. None of our submarines were in the Inland Sea but one of them, code-named "Lifeguard," was stationed at Slippery Sal. They picked up survivors when they could. Generally the pilots had to fly to the sub and ditch beside it to be rescued. Young Ensign George Herbert Walker Bush had already been rescued that way.

But there was no way a U.S. submarine on July 25, 1945, could get into the Inland Sea to rescue Yoder. We were Yoder's only shot at surviving, and he hadn't expected us to be there. He didn't know we had the capability to rescue him. Until we did it, we didn't know it either.

I didn't want to waste time, and with the skill of Crew 5 we hadn't so far. But there had been two emergency radar blips indicating possible survivors. To take Yoder back without searching for a second survivor would mean dooming a man to perish in Japanese capture or alone at sea. We weren't going to abandon the search for him now.

Yoder told us he turned on his emergency IFF signal as soon as he knew he was going down. He hoped his carrier could see his signal on their scope, but he was very low and a long distance away. Yoder thought his buddy saw him go down at the low altitude, the buddy had circled to high altitude above him before he headed towards the carrier. He might have sent a second signal from his higher altitude. The buddy was flying east when Yoder last saw him. That might explain the two blips, but it wasn't enough for us to give up.

Crew 5's job was to search for and rescue survivors of ditched aircraft, so we continued to do the ladder search pattern. We still drew fire from shore batteries. As the afternoon wore on, we could see gun flashes along the shorelines, but no more shells burst around us. Maybe they weren't any more ready to find us flying in this close than Yoder had been.

Warren Smith and his buddy, Ensign J. Gilbert Selway, stayed with us, but the other two of our F6F fighter escort ran so low on fuel that Smith dispatched them back to the Bonhomme Richard. On their way out, the departing fighters were heard to say, "There's those two planes we saw earlier. You take the one on your side, and I'll take this one on my side."

"I got mine — look at that bastard burn!"

"I got the son of a bitch over here, and he's on fire, too!"

Other bits of talk indicated they strafed a few shore installations, then we heard no more. It's possible that this little war they waged diverted Japanese attention away from us the rest of the day.

We continued searching on into the late afternoon. Spotty cloud cover began showing up at 800 to 1000 feet. Warren Smith told us he and Selway had to leave for their carrier, as they had flown with us until they had just enough fuel to get back. Enemy action had dwindled to nil. I told him, "Go ahead. We'll make one more sashay up the Inland Sea and back. Then we'll return to our base in Okinawa."

This could be a bum decision, but I didn't want to leave before finding a survivor if one were there. Sure enough, on our last run up the Sea, Irish spotted a likely object in the water that appeared to be a human being. We landed and taxied back. The object of our search turned out to be a partially submerged section from a small forked tree. It sure looked like a man in the water, limbs spread, till we got right on it.

Now circumstances dictated that I terminate our search for a second survivor. Our fuel was getting low. It was a few minutes before sundown. We took time to let the plane cock around into the wind before revving up for takeoff. For a few minutes we would be sitting ducks on the Inland Sea.

Before we swung around to start the takeoff run of the Willie-7, we saw a Japanese plane coming toward us. He resembled one of our

C47s and was apparently a transport. He was flying at about 800 feet, heading up the Inland Sea toward Kure. Through the overhead window on my side he looked so close I thought I could read the manufacturer's name on his fuselage, "Mitsubishi."

Irish and Willie were our ordnance men, each on a turret. Dale "Gil" Gillings from Madison, Wisconsin, was on the third turret this time.

Gil came to Crew 5 from Patrol Bombing Squadron VP-13, "P" for patrol, out of Kwajalein and Eniwetok. VP-13 had been bombing Japanese island bases that General Douglas MacArthur and Admiral Chester W. Nimitz were going to bypass on the way north out of the South Pacific. Gil had been on long-range search and patrol in PB2Y-3s, the four-engine flying boats. He helped shoot down two Japanese Bettys, our name for their large bombers. While flying over Kusaie in the Caroline Islands, he had a close encounter with a piece of shrapnel that glanced off his helmet and went down his back inside his shirt. An anti-aircraft shell had blown a three-foot hole in the starboard wing and exploded about ten feet above his plane, showering it with hot metal scraps.

Willie, Irish, Gil, and the rest of the crew were itching to cut loose on the enemy this close. The removal of armor plate and additional guns from our PBMs didn't seem such a good idea now as it had on base, but it was done. I had to figure our chances for survival in a fight this far inside the Japanese homeland. I didn't remember exactly how many guns we could expect a Japanese transport plane to have.

What was there in rescue work that entailed further endangering the man we rescued? What good would be our deaths from a fight we picked? What would that do for the pilots going out tomorrow, and the next day, and for the duration?

I'd learned my rules of a gunfight from my Daddy. When I was twelve years old, I was the only one in the family without a paying job to do one day, and the pulpwood cutters needed supervising in our woods. Cutting pulpwood was hard, dirty work, and the men who hired out for it were usually rough customers. Daddy gave me his gun and showed me how to shoot it, in case someone should choose to challenge the owner's son. Daddy said never pull a gun unless I intended to use it. Never use a gun unless I was ready to kill with it.

Sure enough, as the Florida sun rose to high heat that day, a big pulpwood cutter decided that a skinny little boy couldn't make him work anymore. When I called him back to the work, he came at me. I pulled Daddy's gun on him. It was a serious moment.

The cutter didn't have a weapon to match mine. He backed off and went back to work. The next day Daddy fired him.

The lesson certainly stayed with me that pulling a gun on a man was not lightly done. My confrontation with the pulpwood worker had felt like a bluff. It worked because of the traditions that men in his line of work gave way to boys like me who were sons of landowners like my Daddy. Crew 5 of the Willie-7 wouldn't be able to bluff. We didn't know if we had superior fire power over the Japanese transport.

After my experience with the pulpwood cutter, I never wanted to bluff like that again. I'd be willing to shoot in our own defense, but we'd have to be able to win any fight I started.

My gunners requested permission to fire. I said, "No, just watch closely and don't cut loose on him unless he fires. Possibly he hasn't seen us."

We drifted there idling for long moments. Time slowed down to a crawl for me while we waited for the consequences of my decision to withhold fire until fired on.

The transport continued to come on overhead. He was a most closely watched plane. Then we realized, gradually, that he wasn't changing his flight pattern. The attitude of his flight indicated that none of the Japanese on that transport saw us. I never knew why.

FINDING SMITH
AND SELWAY

How glad I was to see that Japanese transport disappear aft! I realized we could breathe now, not sit motionless awaiting our doom.

We took off and headed for our base at Okinawa. Dixie and I were flying. Tuck was navigating. Brownie gave us the report on our fuel supply, and Tuck computed the course back to base. When I heard the numbers, I rubbed the back of my neck with an icy hand. I ordered everyone to throw excess weight overboard.

The heaviest item was our JATO, Jet Assisted Take Off, four bottles of solid rocket fuel I could fire off with an electrical spark to give 12 seconds of burn. Each bottle produced about 3,000 pounds of thrust for its 300 pound weight. Four of them were mounted on the PBM-5, two of them on each after-station door, on each side of the hull well above the water line. We used JATO when we needed extra lift power in open sea takeoffs, in tight spots for taking off in small bays too short to serve as runways for the seaplane, and when we were heavily loaded, for the extra power to shorten the water runway needed to liftoff. But we were headed home. We wouldn't need JATO as much as we needed to lighten up. Airborne and headed back to our base, I couldn't see that we'd need 1200 pounds of JATO anytime soon.

Two hours later, we began to hear a message repeated on the VHF radio, "Red Leader 1, Lifeguard, do you read? Red Leader 1, Lifeguard, do you read?"

Being on VHF, he was probably nearby. I knew that call sign. I could answer the call once without giving anyone much chance to home in on our position. I keyed the mike, "Rebel Yell, Red Leader 1, I'll try to raise Lifeguard for you."

"Red Leader 1, Roger. Slippery Sal."

Thank God for all those "R"s and "L"s in the code name. It was indeed Warren Smith and his buddy Selway. They weren't back to their carrier after all.

Speaking in the same terse radio language, Smith was able to convey to me that they had encountered unbelievably inclement weather between Japan and the Bonhomme Richard. They realized they couldn't stretch their fuel supply enough to get back to their carrier, so they had turned around and flown back to our alliterative rendezvous. At Slippery Sal they had a chance of encountering a U.S. submarine that would surface there from time to time for rescues. This was the "Lifeguard" Warren Smith was trying to raise.

Smith and Selway had stayed with us in the Inland Sea as long as they could. They were in trouble over the open ocean now because they hadn't left us any earlier to conserve their fuel. Our PBM had a better transmitter than their F6F fighter planes, so we took up the call to the submarine.

No answer. We continued to fly toward Slippery Sal. Smith and Selway were circling there.

Again and again, no answer. I expected Red Leader to have another plan to save himself and his buddy. I kept calling Lifeguard.

Still no answer.

Warren Smith came back on the air, "We have only 30 minutes supply of fuel left. Can you land and pick us up when we ditch?"

This was it. I had to make another command decision. No one but me to say yes or no.

I'd been out of contact with our base command since early afternoon. I wasn't about to open up the long range radio now and give the Japanese a chance to home in on us.

There was another danger. If we landed and took off now, we'd never have enough gas to reach the base.

I called Brownie to gather all our men by the interphones. I needed to talk to everybody at once. He passed the word, and they lined up two and three deep at each phone station.

I had been unwilling to risk our lives for a firefight. I wasn't yet ready to risk our lives to pick up Smith and Selway at Slippery Sal. We might raise Lifeguard. But we might not.

I considered landing and takeoff of my seaplane at night. Unsuccessful landings and takeoffs got you killed. In our forward area, there had been only one successful landing and no successful takeoff at night.

We'd have to be awfully lucky. Death in a rescue attempt would be an enemy we couldn't knock out with a .50 calibre machine gun. I took my responsibility of command, but I felt I had to give the crew their choice, to decide what danger to their own lives they were willing to face.

To all the men I said, "We pilots are willing to try a landing and rescue of two fighters who are about to ditch. We know we can land, but taking off may be difficult. If we can't take off, we can still give these men a dry place to sleep tonight. What do you say?"

"Yes. Let's go." All of them said it, just like that. No holding back from a watery grave. True courage. Brave men.

DECIDING TO DIE

Everyone in Crew 5 knew that if Smith and Selway were left to ditch in the night, they wouldn't survive. By morning they would have drifted away from Slippery Sal on their little rafts. No one in any seaplane would be likely to find them then. It would take days for Smith and Selway to die of thirst, starvation, or exposure. Their deaths seemed inevitable if we left them out there alone that night.

I wanted to raise Lifeguard! I didn't want to risk any of us unnecessarily. I keyed the mike, "Red leader 1, I'd rather you ditched and went aboard Lifeguard. I'll be at Slippery Sal in seven minutes. Let's continue calling Lifeguard. When we get to you, we'll decide then."

We reached Slippery Sal in the Willie 7. No one had raised Lifeguard.

When I was little, my Daddy showed me how far to go to save

a man's life. There was a sharecropper family down the dirt road from our homestead. That neighbor family worked for us from time to time, doing the jobs every farm entails. The father came by our house one day during the Depression and said, "Mr. Pasco, you got any work I can do for cash?"

That was an unusual question. Most of us worked in those days for food or barter.

Daddy knew he had plenty of work to do, but he didn't have any cash on hand to pay for it. He asked, "What do you need the money for?"

Our neighbor said, "Mr. Pasco, I got the jaundice. I need to buy my medicine, and the drugstore's gotta have cash for it. I been trying to find some work all over town for money today."

Daddy could see that the man was ill. He said, "You come by our house every day about this time. I'll have some medicine for you when you come by. You won't need to pay for it."

The folk remedy for jaundice was tea made from boiled peach pits, and it was known to work. Daddy and Mama knew how to make the tea so that it wasn't poisonous. The neighbor man agreed to come by our house regularly.

Daddy had just planted a peach orchard from pits he had carefully gathered. They had been hard to come by, and the orchard was our future.

Every morning, Daddy uprooted one of his tiny, precious peach plants for its still visible pit and made the neighbor's tea. Every afternoon, the man came by and drank it. In about three weeks his jaundice symptoms subsided, and a couple of weeks later he was well.

Daddy's little orchard was completely gone. I never heard my folks regret their decision to save our neighbor's life.

Now I couldn't abandon our escort pilots at Slippery Sal. I'd considered all the risks I could imagine. The crew had agreed to what we pilots were willing to do for Smith and Selway. I keyed the microphone.

"Red Leader 1, we'll land and pick you up when you ditch. We're in your vicinity. We'll slow down, turn on our landing lights, and make a 360 degree turn. Watch for us in the sky."

The moon was up about 20 to 30 degrees above the horizon at Slippery Sal. Halfway around our turn, they said they saw us. They came over to us in the air, and we put one on each side of us. I told them to watch when we hit the water and ditch just ahead of us. I gave Smith and Selway these instructions so they would ditch between us and the moonlight glittering on the ocean. It seemed as bright as day in that direction, more than enough light to find them. I planned to see the two little rafts on the shining water, taxi up to each raft, and pull the man aboard.

Then I discovered another difference between flying a land plane and flying a seaplane. Seaplanes skim the water and throw up considerable amounts of spray before they completely settle and stop. Smith and Selway ditched when they saw the keel of our plane kick up the spray but before we had fully landed. They had been eating away at their 30 minutes of fuel in maneuvering for this landing. Whatever the reason, now they were behind us. Looking back, we found no helpful moon glitter as we had ahead of us. Smith and Selway were somewhere back in that cave black darkness.

We turned 180 degrees in the water to taxi back to the downed pilots. We began to get glimpses of their small one-celled flashlights as each man went up on top of the waves in their separate one-man rafts. The inadequacy of their lights could break your heart. They slipped out of sight so often, with ocean swells running about 10 feet now. Everyone on the Willie-7 who could look out was straining to see. We had to stay on some sort of course to get first to one raft, then to the other. We continued to burn gas taxiing toward those dim, bouncing flashes of light.

We finally reached one, then the other raft. The crew pulled each man in to safety in turn. Speed was essential. The engineers and Tuck were checking the plane for damage and leaks. Dixie and I were making ready for takeoff. We had bounced a bit on this landing, but Tuck and I considered it a good landing. There wasn't enough damage to worry us as far as we could tell.

By this time we were like the pig and breakfast — not just involved but committed — when Lifeguard answered our earlier calls. They'd heard us but couldn't respond until they surfaced. I supposed if I could stand to be underwater in a submarine, I'd go deep this close to Japan too. We told them what we'd done.

Then I said, "Do y'all have any aviation fuel aboard? Is there any way you can transfer some to us?"

"No, and no, but you fellows are welcome to come aboard with us."

I had to think about that. We'd landed successfully, but that was no guarantee we would take off without breaking up. I had to be luckier than Harry Widener now.

On the other hand, I really didn't want to get into any submarine. At night. Within 20 miles of Japan. While we were at war with them.

If we got into the air and couldn't make it all the way back to base, I wanted to land on the lee side of one of the islands that string along between Okinawa and Japan. We might be able to trust Naval Intelligence that not all of them were held by the Japanese. We might land about 300 miles from our base when we got down to 30 minutes of fuel.

I didn't find any enthusiasm in the crew or our survivors for going into the submarine.

I thanked Lifeguard and declined his offer. We taxied to face the wind.

It was three hours after dark over Slippery Sal, but the area wasn't in total darkness. The moon was still up above the horizon and shining from the same direction as the wind was blowing. On the surface of the water as we faced the moon, there was on the horizon a line of glitter that had made our landing easier. On takeoff, however, this line was obscured down low in the dark sides of oncoming ocean swells. Each swell loomed as a black void, looking buggerish.

Crew 5 of the Willie-7 had printed instructions on board on how to take-off from the open sea. We had the word of the Coast Guard that their shore experiments showed a seaplane such as ours could do it.

We would be doing it for the first time.

Offshore.

Within 20 miles of the coast of Japan.

At night.

Without JATO, the jet assisted takeoff bottles I'd ditched.

I could taste how badly I wanted the thrust of those 1200 "extra" pounds back on board.

THE VALLEY OF
THE SHADOW OF DEATH

Irish told me years later, "There we were, sitting on the water, and I couldn't swim. I decided I had to get all the life vests straight so we'd all have one when we broke up in the water. It doesn't make any sense now, because we'd probably never know what hit us if we crashed. But I'm down there scrambling, and Lutz stumbles over me."

Lutz chimed in, "I saw you down there on your knees, and I thought you were praying, so I asked, 'Irish, can I pray with you?' I figured a Catholic like you, and me a Lutheran — together we ought to reach Somebody out there."

Irish picked up his story again, "Yeah, so we got down right there and started praying together. First time we'd ever done that, and we've done it ever since."

That night I heard Irish call up to us pilots about then. He told us to get all of us out of there and back home because it was his baby girl's second birthday.

Then Dixie said real soft, like he didn't think it was quiet enough in the plane for Irish and the others to hear, "Sam, what a hell of a time to die, on your kid's birthday."

Dixie surprised me. He didn't have any children, but the way he said it, you might not know that. He could be hard on the men sometimes, but that night he was all on Irish's side about wanting to see his baby again. Our fear made us equals down to our bones.

Picking up Smith and Selway had been the longest 22 minutes

of my life. Now I had to wait for the waves to go through an observable cycle to one we could use to get back into the air. Everyone knew we might die trying.

On the ocean surface, waves come in series. There will be three or four large waves together, then a comparable number of smaller waves, then another three or four large ones. We wanted to start our takeoff run up the front side of the last of a series of large waves, ride down the backside of it, and ride up the front side of the next, smaller, wave. We were supposed to get off the water at that point with sufficient airspeed before the next series of large waves came along.

Waves travel with the wind and at speeds that can be gauged from their height. A 20 foot wave can be travelling in excess of 50 miles an hour, and a 50 foot wave can be travelling several hundred miles an hour. That night, we judged the waves were running 10 feet, between 20 and 30 miles an hour.

All planes take off into the wind, so seaplanes take off into the waves of the sea. Waves push a seaplane backward with a lot of force at takeoff. A wave can toss a seaplane up out of the water before it reaches sufficient flying speed. We had to have a first large wave and a second small one to get this right.

The waves rolled under our keel. I didn't want Irish's baby girl to grow up without a father.

Brownie reported all stations ready for takeoff. Dixie and I were in the pilots' seats; he was on throttles and instruments, and I was on the yoke, rudders, and instruments. Tuck was braced in the doorway between us, watching the instruments too.

We flew a PBM-5 that night. Fifth in the series of seaplanes developed by the Martin Company, it had almost all the bugs worked out, but it didn't allow us to make any mistakes in this situation. We PBY-trained pilots tended to fly PBMs like PBYs and let the noses of a PBM get too low. Then the plane would seem to be at an angle for takeoff but losing altitude — mushing back into the water. I hadn't forgotten that dead pilot in San Diego Bay.

I picked a wave. All the decisions were made now.

We revved up and started our takeoff run on what I believed was the last of a series of large waves. We rode up the front of this, our first wave, and down the backside of it. Gaining speed, good.

We started up the second wave, and it wasn't smaller than the first one after all. Not good. My luck began to run out.

The second wave slowed us down. Worse luck, we weren't up to flying speed. It pitched us into the air.

TOO SOON!

We were in the air without ample flying speed — we were mushing!

Dixie had the throttles and prop pitch fully forward and strained to push them further. I walked the rudders and ailerons to hold us straight and level.

I pulled the yoke back to get as much lift as possible without stalling altogether. I didn't know how much pressure I could still put on the yoke and keep us up out of that black, rushing water. I held the wheel tightly, hanging my plane in the air on its props. I was holding the nose high with all my might, but I didn't know for certain how to avoid a high speed stall.

Tuck softly drawled, "Sam, hold her... Sam, hold her..."

I thought, "Oh, please, God ... if only I knew the precise point to hold the nose of the PBM-5 ... if only I had those JATOS we pitched out four hours ago, if the Pratt and Whitney engines had more horses in them than we knew ... if only the props would push just a little more air for me, if I could get just a little more lift out of the wings Martin gave us on this baby ..."

I was so tense I was cutting button holes in my seat cushion.

The ocean was uncaring of our mortal danger and unforgiving of my choice of swells. The climb-glide indicator showed we were headed down toward the water, not up.

Then our rate of descent began to slow. If we were lucky, it would go to zero. We had to keep from mushing all the way down into the trough between the wave that had tossed us into the air and the next wave ahead of us.

The indicator was slowly coming up to even with the bar, but we were flying level, not up.

The third wave was as large as the first two. Just how unlucky was I going to be this night? All I could see was a black wall of water in front of us. It kept coming at us. We were still mushing.

Slawson at the radio station was breathing, "Oh, no, ... oh, no ...oh, no ..."

Tuck said with more urgency, "Sam, hold her, Sam, hold her."

Yes ... oh, yes ... oh, please ...

WHAM! We hit the crest of the third wave about midship with a thunderously terrific bounce.

The props clawed for air. Tuck and Dixie were both yelling. "The gyro tumbled." "Needle ball and airspeed O.K." "Hold her nose up!"

The gyroscope was whacked out of commission, but my other indicators gave me level readings. The plane was still in the right attitude to get up.

Come on, baby, fly! We were higher above the ocean ...

We were still mushing but not descending as rapidly as before. Airspeed was increasing faster than our descent rate for the first time in this takeoff.

There — a horizon in the moon glitter on the water. I could see over the top of our fourth wave. I could see the next wave behind it. I could see over all the waves ahead. Now I could ease the nose down a little to pick up more speed without losing too much altitude.

Descent rate continued slowing. Mushing ...

Mushing nil ...

Airspeed reached 100 knots. Thank heaven for a working airspeed indicator on this plane. We kissed the crest of the fourth wave with our keel as we climbed out. We were off the water for good!

In the end, luck had nothing to do with it. Irish's invocation held — God was good to us.

GETTING AWAY

We leveled off at 300 feet for fear the Willie-7 was still going to break apart. Dixie recaged the gyro; we couldn't depend on moon glitter to keep the Willie-7 level with the horizon all the way back. Tuck, the engineers, and crew checked the plane over.

We had stationed some of the men in bunks in the bunk room, and others were braced against the bulkhead so as not to get tossed about. Some but not all stations had the wide, heavy seat-belt contraptions we used in those days. The crew were live weight, so we had to check their combined weights at particular stations to balance the plane. We put survivors into the bunks on the lower deck amidships to maintain the plane's center of gravity in the correct spot. We had to ensure that the plane was balanced when all of us crew and pilots were at our stations.

Lt. Smith was a big man, 215 pounds, so he went into one of the lower bunks. When we bounced on the third wave, he was thrown up hard against the upper bunk. He fell back, splitting the heavy canvas bunk stem to stern. A lucky man, Smith wasn't hurt seriously and was still a survivor.

After a few minutes flying, we decided the wings weren't damaged too much — they were still on the airplane. Brownie looked out to see whether the engines were steady, not wobbling, and they looked O.K. Gil reported that the long-range radio aerial had broken loose on that last bounce and was gone. Tuck reported that on a maintenance check of the entire plane no serious damage was found. He and the engineers also went beyond reading the gas meters; they stuck the tanks by hand and figured our gas load. Using the wand by hand this way gave them a figure much closer to our actual load of fuel.

Assured that the plane was flyable, we climbed to a cruising altitude of 8000 feet. We set a course heading of 135 degrees, a southeast direction to separate us from the coast of Japan and head for our base. A straight course to Okinawa would be 180 degrees, putting us right down the shoreline of Kyushu. I wanted to be 100 miles off Japan as soon as possible.

We jettisoned all our expendable gear in order to lighten our load. Everything that wasn't bolted to the plane, or that we didn't need as survival gear for our own use, got the deep six. We threw over everything but the coffee pot and the hot plate. When all our extra brogan shoes went overboard, Irish said, "Tuck, I'm real sorry to see you lose your first pair of real shoes this way."

Gil said, "Mr. Davis, we can't use the long-range radio transmitter without the aerial. It weighs about 300 pounds and is due for a bench test next week. Permission requested to throw it overboard."

"You have my permission. Maybe some sharks down there will bench test it for us."

It felt so great to laugh again with these fellows. I'd nearly killed them.

After about 45 minutes, I felt far enough away from Japan to call on Tuck to give us a steer to Okinawa. Tuck figured we'd flown 100 miles out from Slippery Sal, but he asked me where I thought we were as well. I had no good idea.

I looked at the charts over his shoulder and said, We're ..." I stuck my finger on the chart, "... here."

Tuck plotted our course from that spot, and I hoped to heaven I was right. Dixie asked, "Tuck, do we have enough fuel to get us back to Okinawa?"

The reply came back in that Kentucky drawl, "Why, you fellows didn't have enough gas left to get us back four hours ago!"

That would be about the time we left the Inland Sea with only Yoder. Oh, brother. I called up Brownie, "We're going to have to experiment with the power settings to get the best fuel mixture, RPMs, manifold pressure, airspeed, gasoline flow. We don't know any of this bird's cruise settings."

The PBM-5 was so new to the Fleet that its optimum endurance settings weren't out yet.

Just then Ray Lutz touched me on the elbow. "Mr. Davis," he said, "I don't want to butt in, but let me tell you what happened while I was at HedRon."

Lutz proceeded to tell me the most amazing story. About a month before he left Kaneohe for good to join us, he had engineered for the Pratt & Whitney engine manufacturers to establish power settings for various speeds and endurance on PBM-5s. The settings were top-secret, so Lutz had never mentioned them to anyone else before. With his engineer's head for numbers, Lutz remembered the power setting was 1600 RPM and the manifold pressure was 34.5 inches of Mercury. Then we should lean out the air-fuel mixture until the flame coming from the exhaust stacks had gone just a wee bit beyond blue. There should be a little red fire showing, but not enough to begin burning off the ends of the stacks. We went to those settings without hesitation. I didn't say it to Lutz, but I thought, "The damn thing will fall out of the sky."

THE LAST
TO KNOW

What Lutz didn't tell me then was that he hadn't engineered in those experiments after all. He was at a bar in town when this guy he'd never seen before came up to him and began talking shop. He was the son and grandson, and a nephew too, I think, of Pratt & Whitney engineers. He'd been in on those experiments, and decided for some reason to tell Lutz the secret settings and pressure they'd found.

Lutz told me later that he thought those numbers soun-ded strange, so he didn't tell anyone else. He never saw the guy again, and he didn't have a crew to finagle into testing those settings. It was worse than I thought: he hadn't seen them tried before. He thought I wouldn't use them if I knew how he'd really got hold of them.

He was right.

At the time, Lutz's story reminded me of an old Navy tradition. It seems that John Paul Jones, the first of all Navy officers, was getting bombarded ferociously by the British HMS Serapis. He saw his ship in shambles and about to sink, so he ran it alongside the British attacker. Jones' crew lashed their ship to the Serapis to keep from sinking. Jones ordered hand-to-hand combat.

After about an hour of fierce fighting on the decks of both ships, the British Admiral bellowed on his megaphone, "Are you ready to surrender?"

Admiral John Paul Jones bellowed back, "Surrender, hell, we've just begun to fight!"

One of Jones' marines, bloody and scathed from head to foot yet wielding his blade fiercely, said, "There's always one s.o.b. in the crowd that never gets the word."

We in the field were always the last to get the word. There were only two categories of fighting equipment, obsolete and experimental, but my plane that night was neither.

The Willie-7 didn't fall out of the sky.

In fact, Irish went to the galley to brew up a pot of coffee for all hands. He couldn't do that in a buggy airplane. Our PBM was airworthy.

We were getting closer toward safety, further away from Japan. Everyone was feeling better for getting off the water that last time. Our endurance was stretching.

Life was fine for awhile. Then I began to think how nice it would be to communicate with the base, to send them hourly reports.

Earlier in the day I had ceased all communications with the bases and carriers because we were in Japanese homewaters. All our chatter had been on the VHF interplane radios. The trouble was that lost long-range aerial — we had only short-range radio capability after that big bounce.

We had become our own command, our own little Navy with our own commander-in-chief. All the decisions had been ours alone, no one else to tell us what to do. Up to this point our flight had been successful. Now we were in the air, and I had just had a cup of Irish's coffee.

I wanted back in the Big Navy.

Too Late

We had to get as many miles out of our gas as we could, so Tuck and Brownie set out to drain the hull tanks to the wings. It was a big no-no to drain the tanks completely dry. They had to keep the fuel flowing steady or we'd get an air bubble in the lines.

Tuck worked the hand wobble pump. He and Brownie transferred every drop of fuel to the wing tanks, did it without a vapor lock, and didn't get the plane out of balance the whole time they were doing it. It was an extraordinary feat.

When we began flying with drained hull tanks, we still had a long distance in miles and hours to get back to base. Fuel conservation was important to our survival, so we flew with the plane's nose slightly down.

As our fuel burned, the plane weighed less and less. At the same gas consumption rate, we picked up airspeed little by little.

I had to approach Chimu Wan directly instead of using the secret code approach pattern of July 25th for friendly aircraft. There would be a new code for approach as midnight turned the date to July 26th anyway.

Our radar detector wasn't working properly. We couldn't send out our identification signal because the last big bounce had put it out of commission. When our forces eventually detected us, they would see an unidentified aircraft increasing speed at an angle of attack on an unfriendly approach. We'd look like a Kamikaze on the base radar scopes.

Long overdue, we had no business still being in the air — the power settings were that secret. Whatever our security forces saw on their radar screens, they wouldn't expect it to be the Willie-7.

Without our long-range radio transmitter, I couldn't send our voice code, "Rebel Yell," to our base, "Confederate." The secret code names of all our forces could change at midnight — they did that frequently, without warning. I had only the codes that were in effect when we took off in daylight that morning.

We couldn't be heard on the VHF transmitter until we got within 25 or 30 miles of Okinawa, but I hoped for a skip wave. Sometimes a radio signal hit some phenomenon in the sky and returned to a receiver some farther distance away. So I called, again and again, "Rebel Yell to Confederate. Do you read? Rebel Yell to Confederate. Do you read?"

I kept thinking, "Come on, answer."

At 100 miles out we could hear various communications on the receiver. Every few minutes a call came, "Lairsdale 2 — Cub 9. Do you read? Lairsdale 2 — Cub 9. Do you read?"

Who in the name of heaven was "Lairsdale 2," and who was "Cub 9?"

I dug into the weighted canvas pouch we called "the code sheet" and pulled out the shackle code book. The shackle code didn't change as often as the code names of our bases and units. It gave strange names to insert into radio transmissions, such as calling Kure Naval base "mother's wash pot." I started transmitting longer messages with these code words, and sprinkled speech liberally with the un-Japanese sounds of "R" and "L" — good old "Slippery Sal."

Come on, answer.

At least we didn't fall out of the sky. The trip south kept unfolding slowly before us. Our endurance looked better, but the low level warning lights came on for one tank, then another, and another — I hated those little lights as each one winked on.

Come on, answer.

It was quiet enough for me to wonder what the base commanders were thinking. I imagined Bonvillian, our C.O., regular Navy and an Annapolis ring-knocker, pacing the deck and muttering about me, "That jg has killed our first crew and lost our first plane. A good record ruined!"

VH-3 had a perfect record of recovering flyers without loss of life or planes. Bonvillian himself had taxied a crippled PBM for 26 hours, over 250 miles back to base, rather than radio for help and have to ditch the plane when help arrived. With only six planes in the squadron, we had to make do like that.

Come on, answer.

Tuck plotted and replotted our course. We had avoided Amami O Shima with its intense, accurate Japanese fire-power. But we had to face our own base defense forces on Ie Shima. Base security had every right to blow us out of the sky.

I kept calling. Come on, answer.

I was more afraid of our forces shooting us down now than I had ever been of the Japanese. I worried about security's frustration with our radio silence. I felt sure that the heavy guns' gunners wanted to fire on the Willie-7 in fulfilling their duty to protect and defend our base.

Come on, answer.

"Rebel Yell to Confederate. Do you read?" I kept my voice calm. I would not reveal my anxiety to the crew or the base. But in my head the litany of fear and hope continued:

Come on, answer ... answer... answer ... For God's sake, ANSWER.

THE GUNS OF IE SHIMA

Over the bow of the plane, we could see Ie Shima outlined in phosphorus. Any other time it would have been beautiful, but the big guns down there weren't going to let us get past them.

FINALLY, 35 miles out from Chimu Wan and 5 minutes off Ie Shima, the base jigged me for positive identification. They heard us on the VHF at last!

I answered them with the codes we still had from that morning. The base didn't seem satisfied. Oh great, the codes must have changed at midnight, now of all times.

They jigged me again for shackle code identification. Now I put nonsense words into a code that might communicate who we were — "We're Crew 5 of the Willie-7 playing Victor Herbert's 3rd symphony, and we all have old colds in our noses from dancin' with Slippery Sal."

Please God, let somebody down there remember our own name for ourselves.

Their silence stretched for an eternity.

Security would never let an unfriendly craft get past them. I didn't have enough gas to circle outside the big guns' range. Our only hope was clearance from our base at Chimu Wan.

Ie Shima was five miles ahead ... two minutes flying time ... please, base, recognize us.

One more minute ... please, base ...

Please, please ...

"Lairsdale 2 clears Crew 5 of the Willie 7 to straight in approach."

I said, "No."

STRAIGHT IN

I heard Dixie say, "Oh, shit. This is it now, an intercept."
He seemed ready to kill me himself, but I had to think about crashing, now, so close to safety. A straight in approach put us over the south end of Okinawa, an area too big to glide over. All the low level lights were lit by then, even both wing tanks. Running completely out of gas was imminent. I had to stay over water.

"Crew 5 of the Willie-7 will round the point and turn straight in over the pass to Lairsdale 2."

No silence, no argument. They cleared us for my approach. Now all we had to do was execute it.

Past Ie Shima, we rapidly closed in on Chimu Wan. The 25 miles between them would take about ten minutes. Hold on, you sweet old plane. Dear God, hold on.

We got round the point. Thank you, God, for phosphorus in the waters down there — I could see the pass.

Through the pass and still flying — I could hear the engines drone.

Come on, baby, we're almost there. I lowered the flaps. We lost more altitude.

The keel touched the bay at Chimu Wan. The spray arched higher around us as we slowed and settled into that blessed water. We bounced just a little ...

We were down. All of us. In one piece! Safe! I was never so happy in all my life to be back on the water.

THE BIG NAVY

We could still taxi, so I headed for the mooring buoy in Chimu Wan. Of all the buoys that guided me all my life, this was the most beautiful one I'd ever seen. I relished the thought that once more Willie would pick up Irish and hold him out the plane door like a living boat hook to secure us to that gorgeous buoy.

Fifty yards short of the buoy, the port engine quit. We didn't cross over fuel from the starboard tank to restart the engine — its tank was dry.

We threw out another sea anchor on the starboard side to keep from running in circles. Willie and Irish might have to wait.

I called for a launch to come to our aid. Back in my instructor days I had skimmed across Corpus Christi Bay rather than have my cadets see me being towed. Now I didn't care about the ignominy of it. I was relieved just to call for help and get it.

Having been spared our lives, we were spared even ignominy that night. The extra sea anchor steered the plane enough that we reached the buoy. Willie and Irish went into their human boat hook routine after all.

Irish locked her up with the line in his hands, running it through the ring in that wonderful buoy and thrusting it back to another crew member to snub it to the bow post. They yelled up to the pilot's seat, "Buoy made."

I sighed with utter relief. Brownie asked just then, "Did you guys cut the starboard engine?"

"No."

"I didn't either, but it's quit too." The starboard engine at that moment totally consumed the last drop of 2600 gallons of gas. We had made it safely to base with all hands aboard, arriving six hours overdue and four hours beyond our gas supply for regular flight.

Now we wondered if we were in or out of the Navy.

The launch arrived and took us to the Pine Island. When we came alongside the gangway, someone who sounded like Capt. William L. Erdmann, commander of all Air-Sea Rescue forces in the area, yelled, "Do you have your survivor?"

I wondered what he thought we'd been doing out there all this time. We weren't about to be the first in VH-3 to leave survivors behind if we could help it. I yelled back, "Yes, sir. We have three." Cheers came from the bridge. We were still in the Navy after all.

MUDDY WATERS

The pilots and survivors were called into the ward room of the USS Pine Island for debriefing. The rest of Crew 5 was met by the Officer of the Day and informed they were late for buoy watch. Three men and a pilot had to stay on each seaplane at night. Many times Japanese saboteurs swam out to damage or sink our planes on the water, but the brass could have handled the guarding of our plane differently that one night. They didn't.

In the ward room we met with Capt. Erdmann, Lt. Cdr. Waters acting as his chief of staff, and what seemed like all the rest of Erdmann's staff. It was crowded.

I had figured out by then that "Lairsdale 2" was the new code name for our base, and "Cub 9" was the new name for us on the Willie 7. In the debriefing, I learned the other side of the story. Base Security had been tracking us for several hours. They had orders to fire on us when we passed abeam of Ie Shima.

Muddy Waters stayed in the communications shack control room all those hours. He thought maybe the hostile unidentified aircraft was us. He wanted to believe we were still in the air, though we were far too long overdue for it to be us. But he didn't stop hoping, and he didn't leave the shack.

Waters' wait stretched through the night hours and into the earliest morning, all the time we were picking up Smith and Selway, getting off the water by moonlight, ditching our weight, and conserving gas on the secret power settings. He knew only that we were overdue, that a lone aircraft was headed his way, and just maybe we'd all get lucky.

Finally my voice came into the shack over the VHF. Waters reacted instantly —

"HOLD OFF! Hold your fire! I'd know that country boy's voice in Hades. That's a friendly coming in — notify our forces not, I repeat, not to fire on that target!"

When I heard Waters tell that, all the risks, the danger, the unvoiced fears came flooding back.

I had been allowed to fly past Ie Shima because of the hope in this one man. We had lived at last because of the courage of his convictions. In front of all that brass, I choked up. I still do.

DADDY'S
THIN LINE

C apt. Erdmann gave us an early breakfast and told us to hit the sack for some sleep. There would be aspects of intelligence to discuss later in the day. I went back to my bunk. I was back in the Big Navy. Doubts crowded my pillow, and I couldn't sleep.

I wondered if this next session was the time they dressed me down for taking the whole thing into my own hands? For not contacting the base all afternoon and night? For risking the plane landing and taking off for Smith and Selway rather than waiting for the submarine to take them on? For not getting into that infernal submarine?

I kept having cold chills originate along my belt line. They reverberated along my neck and cheeks and disappeared off the top of my head. I was keyed up higher than ever before.

The sun came up while I tossed about trying to catch some sleep. At daylight, Brownie and Lutz checked the Willie-7 to see if our last ferocious bounce had buckled the spars. What they found were two wrinkles bulged up, running fore and aft on the skin of the hull, on each side of the hull at the top where the wings joined it. Our fears weren't unfounded that after that last bounce the wings might fall off. There was more.

Salt water had damaged our propellers. The leading edge of the lower halves were badly pitted, and about four inches of the tips were pitted away. If they had pitted unevenly, we would have lost balance of the plane. We would have fallen out of the sky after all.

And more. One of our engines had 800 hours of operation on it and would normally have been replaced in a few hundred more flight hours. Brownie and Lutz found we had only 13 gallons of oil left in that engine. Another hour of operation and it would have frozen up and quit from lack of oil. We must have laid an oil streak from Slippery Sal to Okinawa.

And when we leaned out the fuel mixture on Lutz's settings, we had to get a few sparks in the exhaust, but not too many sparks. The ends of the stacks normally burned off a little on takeoff, climb, and high speed. The exhaust stacks had to be replaced every 200 hours in rough use. Brownie and Lutz saw that the stacks of the Willie-7 had to be replaced before she went back into service.

So after giving up my nervous attempts to sleep, I heard about all this damage to our plane. I knew the Navy didn't think highly of abusing equipment or unduly risking men in this war. I remembered my Daddy's idea that there's a real thin line between a hero and a damn fool. On which side of the line did the Navy think I was now?

Yoder being a Hoosier, Leo M. Litz from The Indianapolis

News came over to get the story. Litz had come out to cover news of Hoosiers in the war, and already knew Capt. Erdmann from Greensburg, Indiana.

Litz published a picture of Warren Smith, Selway, Yoder and me in the sunlight on deck. Selway and Yoder look content. Warren Smith has a serious set to his jaw. I have wrinkles on my forehead and my eyebrows knit in an anxious manner — I was one worried country boy that morning.

I entered the ward room again late in the afternoon July 26, 1945. I had wondered about the delay. This was it. My Daddy's thin line.

The ward room filled up before I got there. There were a lot of brass — Generals, Colonels, Admirals, Commanders — and Yeomen. All those uniforms — Army, Navy and Marine Corps. Whatever happened next, I'd have an audience.

I waited to be asked for intelligence. The questions were everything I could think of, and then some more would be put to me and the others. We were set to spotting on the maps, pointing out areas where we saw gun flashes on the shoreline. Every little detail interested our inquisitors: mooring areas, boat slips, shoreline topography, air fields. We had noted a number of damaged and broken ships — more grist for the mills they were grinding exceedingly fine.

We were asked what type of aircraft was shot down. Smith said, "We don't know, but from the transmissions we heard, one was a bastard and the other was a son of a bitch."

The questions proceeded from me, Dixie, Tuck, Yoder, Smith, and Selway, to several other rescued survivors who had collected on the Pine Island. It always took awhile for their transportation to the various carriers to get underway. All these survivors and the pilots from VH-3 not flying that day were queried in turn as closely as I was.

We knew we were being asked for any scrap of information that could be useful in future briefings of all our forces. We had all been in Japanese waters. As our forces had neared their homeland, we believed the Japanese had become more doggedly determined to fight to the last man. Iwo Jima and Okinawa, the last two embattled islands between Japan and the South Pacific, were fresh in our minds. We expected ferocious determination when we fought the whole population on their sacred homeland. We had to give our forces every possible detail that we could remember, accurate and to the point.

Eventually the questions seemed to be coming to an end. Capt. Erdmann stood up. He put his hand on my shoulder and looked at Lt. Cdr. Bonvillian.

"Bonny, I want you to write to Admiral Halsey recommending this man for the Navy Cross. Send it through me. I'll endorse it and send it on to Halsey."

No court martial. That felt good. Another man stood in the briefing room and spoke.

"This is some good news coming down the pike. We can take this back to our units and tell them we can rescue them anywhere, anytime. They no longer have to take off for sorties in Japan on a one way street."

That felt better.

Other voices chimed in. They said knowing Air-Sea Rescue was this capable would be the "greatest boost to morale that had ever been instigated." We were praised highly for "exerting initiative."

Bonvillian muttered that his crews had been doing this all along. I agreed. VH-3 pilots had for several months done the almost impossible in racking up rescue feats. What we were doing felt routine. I was proud to be part of an outfit that valued a human life so much that we'd send 11 PBM crew members, 4 fighter pilots, and 5 planes (worth a total of $410,000 in those days) to rescue one of us inside Japan alone. We were all — pilots, crews, ship's tender personnel, maintenance people — just doing our jobs.

That felt best of all.

ENOUGH GAS

C rew 5 of the Willie-7 went back on duty, one day off, two days on. Pilots bombed and strafed Japan, and continued to ditch; VH-3 picked up survivors. Our successful landing and takeoff of a seaplane at night went into the Navy sea annals. Once it was done, and publicized out there with the Navy Cross recommendation, others did it too. We rescued survivors "anytime, anywhere."

On August 1, 1945, we flew the squadron out from Okinawa to Saipan to avoid a typhoon. When we took off, the winds were gusting at 35 to 40 knots, and ocean swells were rolling into Chimu Wan. I gratefully used JATO to take off.

When we arrived at Saipan 11.5 hours later, the skipper said to gas up to 1800 gallons. I told Brownie, "Put in another 200 gallons for Mary Lona."

The typhoon was clocked at 20 miles an hour, so the skipper decided we'd go back the next night to arrive shortly after dawn. We got to our plane about 2200 hours to find we would be towed out beyond myriad seaplanes that blocked us in. After much squabble with operations and launch coxswains, we finally got unmoored, started, and ready for takeoff. I called on Brownie to give us the gas load, to run it on the loading scale, so we could station ourselves around the plane for balance on takeoff. I was amazed to learn all our tanks were full, 2600 gallons.

I said, "Brownie, you really gave us extra gas."

He said, "Well, you said you wanted 200 for Mary Lona, and I put in 200 for my Ruth, then Irish came by and thought Sheila needed 200, and Willie's girl needed 200."

And of course the last 400 extra gallons were for Evelyn Dicken and one of Dixie's cousins. I didn't even have to ask.

THE BEGINNING
OF THE END

At Okinawa we went on air raid alerts almost every night. During raids our security forces smoked in the seadrome, sending floating cans of burning chemicals onto the water to blow evil-smelling smoke over the bay.

When the bay was "smoked in," the attackers saw fog rather than all our planes, ships, buildings, and men below.

Occasionally Japanese soldiers swam out to our planes anchored on the water and tried to sink them. Our buoy watches posted on each plane had to be alert. One man on watch saw a smoke can floating upwind and blasted it with his .45 calibre tommy gun. The can, and whatever was making it float, sank.

We all talked about the war winding down to victory for us. The Japanese still sent one or two Kamikaze aircraft at a time to Okinawa, instead of eight or ten they had sent several weeks before. I visited my cousin Paul Redmond on his LCI-G, a landing craft converted to a rocket ship in close support of the invasion forces. There was still fighting in the northern and mountainous parts of the island, but Paul's landing craft were no longer used. Our assaults on Okinawa beaches were over.

Lt. Warren Smith said he thought something was about to happen. "Sam, there were some highly classified doings happening at Berkeley while I was there. I believe our people will crack the atom before this war is over."

Years later, I learned that when Smith and I were in the Inland Sea July 25th, President Harry S. Truman issued the general order to proceed with the plan to use the atomic bomb on the Japanese cities of Hiroshima, Kokura, Niigata, or Nagasaki. The day before at the Potsdam Conference, Truman told Josef Stalin of the Soviet Union that the U.S. had the atom bomb, and Stalin hadn't acted surprised.

On July 26, 1945, President Truman, the new Prime Minister Clement Atlee of Great Britain, and Generalissimo Chaing Kai-shek of China issued an ultimatum to Japan from Potsdam, to surrender unconditionally or suffer "the utter destruction of the Japanese homeland." I did not know at the time that the same day the USS Indianapolis delivered the U-235 portion of an atomic bomb to the north Pacific island of Tinian.

Hiroshima was hit with one atomic bomb August 6, 1945. The news of destruction was horrifying, but no less so at the time than what we expected to endure invading Japan. The road back to the Inland Sea from Pearl Harbor for our forces had been long, costly, bloody, and perilous every inch of the way. It had taken us more than three years to be within flight range of the Inland Sea of the Japanese homeland. We weren't out of danger yet.

VH-3 had been called forward in 1943 and Crew 5 of the Willie-7 had been formed in 1944 to support the invasion of Japan itself. Now in 1945 we had our orders to form up the squadron on August 13, 1945, for invasion. The last assault on Japan would be all that had gone before, and more. It came down to us or them, the Allies or the Japanese.

As the atomic bomb was death to Hiroshima, it was a harbinger of life for us.

OLD #59081

On August 9, 1945, VH-3 ordered Crew 5 to fly to the north shore of Shikoku, standby, and open sealed orders out there at 1000 hours. One of the pilots and three other crew members of Crew 5 slept each night as buoy watch on our Willie-7 of the moment. Keeping watch over the plane didn't seem such a brass hat trick as it had earlier. The rest of us arrived to take off at daylight.

The briefing officer revealed to us that another atomic bomb was to be dropped, and we were to standby for rescue. We flew to the north shore of Shikoku, arriving at our station on time. The sealed orders told us to standby for Air-Sea-Rescue if weather permitted Kokura to be bombed. No one ditched for us to find.

We kept watch to see the mushroom shaped cloud, but did not see it. When we returned to base we learned that the bomb was dropped on an alternate target on the west side of Japan — Nagasaki.

When we tethered to our buoy in Chimu Wan, the launch came alongside with a new crew for the plane. The launch commander said, "Don't secure anything. We'll gas up and go. There's a typhoon coming this way, and we're evacuating everything we can to Saipan. All of you go aboard the Pine Island."

Everybody hustled. All but two of our seaplanes were flyable and being flown to Saipan. Crews dashed about getting their planes ready. The ship's crew scurried around preparing to go to sea. For seaplane tenders and other ships it was better to weather a storm underway in the open sea rather than stay to be tossed about in a harbor.

One of the seaplanes was up on the fantail of the Pine Island undergoing hull repairs, so it was tied down more securely. The other unflyable plane was #59081, tethered to a buoy while repairs were in progress on its port engine. We got a cherry picker barge, a barge with a crane on it, to pull up another buoy to double up the mooring. Usually a seaplane was tethered to one buoy by the bow pennant, a 3/8 inch cable, and both bow doors were closed. In doubling up that day, we attached the second buoy to the bow post inside the plane. Then we attached the first buoy to the bow post from the other side. This required both bow doors on the plane be left open.

When we got #59081 double moored, we went aboard ship and put out to sea. I was on a ship underway at sea for the first time, and here I was in a typhoon. Our sleeping quarters were way below decks in the bow of the Pine Island. I found I could do better on the upper deck at midships in the salt spray.

The entire Navy flotilla from Okinawa put to sea with us and maintained formation by sight and by radar. The ocean swells grew larger as the wind velocity increased. The destroyer escorts fared the worst. They pitched and rolled, bow down, bow up, from side to side. They rode high on the crests, then sank in the trough completely out of sight. The long seconds before I could see them again from the Pine Island seemed like an eternity. We wallowed out the typhoon all night and the next day. By luck, or craft, or the grace of God, we lost no men, damaged no ships.

All day August 10th we listened to Japanese commercial radio. We heard a very forceful voice making speeches in Japanese. I caught only two English words, "Potsdam" and "Truman," and he said them often all day. I thought he might try to prepare the Japanese people to call for peace. I believed that would be a real turnaround for them, as we understood they told their people all along that they were still winning the war.

The storm subsided enough at 1400 hours that we headed back to Okinawa. When we steamed into the seadrome area on Chimu Wan, marvel of marvels, old #59081 was still afloat. We expected it to be in the deep six still tethered to the buoys. The bottom of the bow doors was only two inches above the water. If someone poured an eight ounce glass of water into the plane it would surely sink. Crew 5 was scheduled to fly it at daylight the next day — it was to be our next Willie-7.

As maintenance officer of the squadron, I called on Fleet Air Service Squadron (FasRon) maintenance to hurry up the engine repairs. Crew 5 had to pump the plane out and clean it up for flight. We didn't dare let the slightest weight upset the plane and sink it. We ran a launch alongside with a pump and a suction hose to pump out most of the water before we boarded her. The engine crew wound up their repairs at daybreak.

The FasRon crew chief came to the pilot seat with the story of what happened in the first place. This plane had come in with a top jug — a cylinder — shot out. They were replacing it when we went to sea. They stuffed a big rag in the hole, but in the storm it either blew away or went down into the engine. When they got back to it, the engine was full of water.

He said, "We screwed out the spark plugs on all the lower cylinders, let the water drain out, and put in new plugs. We probed down in the engine, but we couldn't hook onto the rag. We think it must have blown away. We'll stay aboard until you get the engines running, then we'll get in the launch and go back to the ship.

"If I were you, I'd give this engine a good test run on the water at full power until you're satisfied it'll hold full power before you take off."

Oh yeah.

Back out of the war zone where we had more time, we would have test hopped this repair, then checked the oil sump before going into service. As it was, the test hop was our first hour out toward Bungo Suido to cover a B-25 bombing raid of Kure and Hiroshima. She ran fine.

We liked old # 59081. The PBM-5 was just an excellent plane.

WAR'S END

Out there the next day, August 12th, word came unofficially from Japanese radio that peace was at hand. Some of us on Okinawa and at Chimu Wan had portable radios. When the peace feeler was broadcast, about half the base on land and sea started celebrating. That wouldn't have been so bad, except they chose to fire tracers, star shells, and flares in their happiness. Into the air, of course, not horizontally at each other. They played with the searchlights, just to celebrate our good fortune, sort of an opening night for peace.

The buoy watchers on the sea planes didn't hear the rumor, so they thought all the firing meant we were under attack. They went on alert and waited for our security forces to smoke in the bay. When the air remained clear, they figured out something less deadly was up.

Some units went on cease fire; some did not. Officially, our security forces remained alert and ready. It was just as well. Two Kamikaze flights came into Okinawa just after dark August 12th.

Tokyo Rose and her misinformation were back on the air that night. She said through much static, "Two brave kamikaze pilots sank the Pine Island at Okinawa. Oh, you poor dear boys on the Pine Island, we are so sorry for your folks. They should not have sent you to Okinawa. You poor, cold, shivering troops in the mud and the water getting pinned down, getting killed, being lonely so far from home. Wouldn't you rather be in your nice warm dry bed at home in the arms of your wives? You have lost the war. You should give up and go home."

At the time, I was having fried chicken and hot coffee with all hands alive on the Pine Island. Japanese broadcasts still lied to everyone.

On the 13th of August, we got the squadron ready to move to Saipan. Three crews left just before dark: Crew 5; Lt. jg W.P. "Pop" Randall, the old-timer in our squadron who was older than Tuck and me; and Jim Blumenstock, another PPC in the squadron. We intended to rendezvous at 8,000 feet and fly together.

Pop Randall took off first and started his climb up over Okinawa. As we were making our takeoff run next, the General Quarters signal went up; I continued on up. This was no victory celebration. Security began to smoke in the bay, so Blumenstock couldn't take off. He had a most difficult time taxiing back to the buoy in the smoke. You could lose your plane and your life in a crowded seadrome.

The wind was such that Randall and I climbed over Buckner Bay to the south of Chimu Wan. I heard on my radio that the USS Pennsylvania had been hit, but the battleship didn't appear to me to be damaged much. I had the clearer view that they were smoking in Buckner and firing at everything that moved in the air. I called him, "Pop, Buckner's under attack. Get out of there!"

Crew 5 immediately took our Willie-7 down to running 100 feet above the water. I blessed the memory of the fabulous Fondren who taught me exactly how to judge where the keel of my 50 foot high seaplane was at all times. Twenty miles out from Okinawa, we rose to 8,000 feet, and I called Pop to rendezvous out there. He was still over Buckner Bay at 8,000 feet, waiting for me. He hadn't understood my call to him. I couldn't believe he hadn't been picked off yet by our own radar aimed guns. This time I made sure he understood my message, and we both got out of there.

The night wasn't over for us yet. We had to cross the weather front usually hanging about two-thirds of the way from Okinawa to Saipan. Slawson tuned up the radar, and we picked our way around the thunderheads, "thunder bumpers," for awhile. On the radar screen we saw two squall lines lying to each side of us with a clear area between them. Of course we went into the clear area.

Twenty minutes later, a horseshoe shaped target came up on the screen, dead ahead of us. The whole screen shortly went white with so many targets that their blips blended together in a mass. The wind got terrific; rain and hail pounded us ferociously. Before I could think, the plane shot up from 7,000 to 11,500 feet. The cylinder head temperature dropped rapidly. The engines began cutting out; I thought they were icing up.

We tried to push the nose of the plane over enough to go down, but the airspeed indicator showed we were over 200 knots. I didn't dare exert any more air pressure on the wings. The instruments fogged up. We shivered in our flight jackets. The gyro horizon tumbled. Cold and alert, we hung on.

It took us ten minutes to get back down to 7,000 feet the first time. Then another vertical current took us up again. For some time this weather system buffeted us, up, down, and sideways. When we weren't hurled entirely up or down, vertical air currents lifted or depressed one wing. The plane turned almost on its side, and we'd have to wrench her around every time.

Eventually we got through this weather, but we were blown several miles north off course before we broke into the clear. This time I could send "M"s and "O"s to the base on Saipan; they got a bearing on us and confirmed our navigation position. Of course, Tuck and Dixie once again navigated rather than trusting to my rusty calculations. Good for them, and for us.

We altered course. We made Saipan as planned.

*Above left: Sam and Mary Lona "In love, on horseback", enjoying a
second honeymoon in San Diego, before goodbyes,
Above right: Sam, defying gravity at Mission Beach*

*Above: Crew 5 and their wives enjoying time together at Mission Beach
before the men shipped out for duty in the Northern Pacific.*

Carroll Wilson   Raleigh Slawson   Dale Gillings   Robert Gibson   Sam Davis   Richard Ronstrom   Mervin Dicken   John Reid

Gordon Petersen   Don Flaherty   Harry Brown   Ray Lutz

Crew 5 of the Willie-7

Sam, in the driver's seat

Above and below: Pearl Harbor in reverse. All the Japanese ships that were involved in the attack on Pearl Harbor were eventually sunk by U.S. forces.

Lower right: The heavy cruiser Tone was sunk at Kure on July 28th, 1945, by U.S. carrier planes.

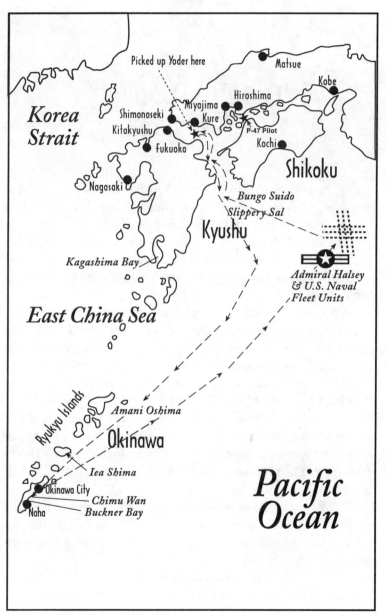

Our route to the inland sea

THE C.O. ACCEPTS
A SURRENDER

B etween August 15 and September 4, 1945, the rest of VH-3 joined us on Saipan, and Bonvillian had a change of duty from being our C.O.

Lt. Cdr. Jeff Kennedy became our squadron commanding officer. He was from New York and real gung-ho on being regular Navy. We were in transition because our preparation to invade Japan went on hold.

A day or two later, VH-3 sent a command party — Admirals, government officials, our C.O. — down to the island of Truk to accept the Japanese surrender there. Truk was a strong base for the Japanese. The Allies had decided not to take it, even though we needed it. Our forces bypassed Truk on our march north across the Pacific from New Guinea. We surrounded it, isolated it, and used Ulithi Island as our base instead. Now Lt. Cdr. Kennedy would be part of the surrender of Truk without the awful loss of American life on so many other islands. It was a major highlight for VH-3 to participate. The next day, August 14, 1945, Japan surrendered. It wasn't a minute too soon for me.

The first thing Kennedy did on his return to Saipan was call a staff meeting. Pacing the floor in front of us, he said, "Men, we have some work to start immediately, in fact, beginning within ten minutes of this meeting.

"I have been many places in the Navy, and when the Old Man flew anywhere, the men always rolled out the best ship, and the best crew, to take him. I believe you men are the same as any other. So you gave me the best you have to fly to Truk.

"If that's the best, then WHAT IN THUNDER ARE THE REST

OF YOU FLYING?" The first thing I noticed was that many of the aluminum deck plates were cracked and broken. Some were missing. I had to be extremely careful where I stepped."

Well, yes, we were in a war zone, and we were Depression kids grown up. We lived and flew by the motto of make do or do without.

There was more from Kennedy. "A few hours out, I asked Chuck about the navigation. He was using dead reckoning. I asked about Loran. Chuck said there was no cross station available, and he could get only one line. So I asked about the octant to get a sun line for a cross check on the Loran line.

"They searched the plane over and found one in the bunk room underneath some haphazardly piled life jackets. They opened it up, and it was an empty box.I asked about drift, and Chuck looked out the pilot's window. He said, 'Yes, it's ... five degrees left."

Ensign Charles Scarborough was a good navigator. Kennedy continued, "I asked Chuck, 'Where did you get that?'

"He said, 'The wind is 15 knots off the starboard bow.' I asked, 'Have you *read* the drift?'

"He said, 'The stovepipe drift is inoperable. They were in our way, sir, doing rescue, so we plugged up the well and stored the pipe in the Quonset Hut on Saipan.'

The stovepipe drift sight was a big, bunglesome piece of equipment. I thought some engineers dreamed it up when they had nothing better to do in the war effort. It had to be expensive. We all had experience with the stovepipe drift sight.

In San Diego Crew 5 had come in from a flight, beached our PBM, and parked it on the apron. When we headed for the hangar, one of us asked, "What's that wire doing hanging from the afterstation, there, underneath the hull?"

I took a look to find it was a sundered wire that controlled a prism in the bottom of the stovepipe. The pipe went through a well in the bottom of the hull. When extended in use, the whole contraption stuck about three feet below the plane's hull, sort of like an upside down periscope. We had obviously left it in operational place instead of picking it up prior to landing. The pipe broke off smooth with the hull when we landed.

From then on, Crew 5 used a simple little $35 polaris to read wind drift through the open tunnel hatch.

Kennedy must have had the same thought. He said, "Then I asked Chuck if they had a polaris. They found one in a box near the auxiliary generator. It was frozen up with salt water corrosion, so no one could use it.

"Chuck was confident that we were on course and would hit the ETA properly. Which I might add, we did.

"However, beginning today, all you patrol plane commanders get your planes in tip-top shape.

"DISMISSED!"

Yes, sir. The war was over.

TALES OF THE NORTH PACIFIC

We were like captive tourists on Saipan.

We foraged for papayas and bananas, of which there seemed to be an unlimited supply. The best ones were up in the hills. It was an adventure to hunt for so much bountiful fruit. We finally had more bananas than Crew 5 could consume in a day.

The land gave every evidence of fierce battle — old fox holes in the coral rock and what little soil there was on the island. I found one hole with the bones of five people in it. I never knew whether they were us or them.

Not every Japanese soldier was dead on Saipan. We had movies outdoors at night. Everybody usually wore a poncho and a pith helmet. One night before the war was over, the projector had to be adjusted, so they turned on the lights before the movie finished. The Master of Arms saw three soldiers who were barefooted. When he went over to tell them they should wear their shoes at all times, he realized they were Japanese.

Not every Japanese soldier surrendered after the war either. Some of them up in the hills fired on a bunch of us exploring there one day. We lost our taste for bananas in the hills after that.

We did a lot of skin diving and fishing on the reefs in the lagoon. There were jillions of small and large multi-colored tropical fish swimming in and out of the coral rock. It was pure joy to swim about them with a mask on.

One day I came from the kitchen with some meat for bait, to get Tuck to go fishing with me. When I found him, he was wearing his good khaki uniform, new shoes and all. I had my swim trunks on. I promised Tuck he could stay in the boat, and I would be careful not to get him wet.

I walked along in shallow water pulling Tuck in a rubber life raft we retrieved from one of the survivors we picked up from Okinawa. Back home, I always liked to fish the bottom of a shallow bay, and here I was halfway around the world from home still doing it.

We arrived at the reef's edge and fished there awhile. Tuck and I kept saying if we had fish for bait, then we could catch some fish. With no luck, we finally started back in.

Pulling the boat, I walked up on a small coral boulder with many tropical fish minnows running in and out of its holes. I wiggled it loose from the bottom and shook it over the boat. Numerous little fish fell out of the rock.

We were jubilant that we had good bait and exclaiming over our good luck when a moray eel fell out of the rock into the raft. He looked ferocious, wriggling around with his mouth popping open. Tuck jumped out of the raft into knee deep water, good uniform, shoes and all.

I'd managed to ruin the second pair of real shoes I think my country-boy buddy ever had.

Occasionally I rode around the island in a weapons carrier. We were based at Tanapang Harbor, on the west coast about midway down the island. Our military had a road up the mountain spine of Saipan and across onto the eastern shore.

Coming down the mountain on the east side there was a sharp turn around a harbor bay about 150 feet below the road where the cliff was sheer. While we were on Saipan, someone went around that turn too fast in a jeep. It rolled over, threw everyone out, and fell off the cliff into the bay. They got the crew's cherry picker crane to come grapple up the jeep.

The crane pulled up a jeep. It wasn't their jeep, so they grappled again. That day they pulled out three jeeps, a weapons carrier, and two Japanese trucks before they quit.

I visited Tinian, where the B-29 fleet took off to bomb Japan. I went up to Marpi Point where thousands of Japanese troops and noncombatants jumped off the cliff to their deaths rather than surrender to our Marines.

I felt the after effects of war — glad to be alive in all the destruction around me.

PETS

There were two pets on Saipan, a dog and a nanny goat. I especially liked the goat. She reminded me of home. Our goats in Farmdale were the old Spanish common breed like my nanny goat on Saipan. Our Florida goats roamed the open range. Whereas our cattle ranged in a 20 to 40 mile radius, our goats ranged over about 5 miles. My first job in the family was to herd our goats with my brother Carl.

Goats are a low maintenance animal and can thrive on very little care. Most of the time ours came home at night where we had a goat house and gave them a small amount of feed. These old Spanish goats acted like natural pets. It was no surprise to me that "my" nanny goat survived the war on Saipan.

Goats multiply rapidly. Nanny goats usually give birth to two kids, and it's not uncommon for them to have triplets. Occasionally our goats had four kids at a time, and rarely only one. The mother goats hid their kids in the bushes and seemed to forget where they were. Carl and I watched the goats closely in the Spring when the kids were born.

We carried four or five burlap sacks when we followed the goats out of the goat house on Spring mornings. We didn't force them in any particular direction. They gave birth in the woods, then before the nanny could hide the kids in the bushes, we picked them up. Croker sacks, gunny sacks, mullet sacks, or burlap sacks were good to carry live animals in because they could breathe through them.

We couldn't put but one nanny's kid in each sack. Should we put two in one sack, the nannies refused to nurse any of the kids. Putting them together mixed up their odors for the mothers. We always washed the sacks and dried them in the sun before we used them again.

I was only on Saipan for six weeks, and it wasn't springtime. All I did was feed the goat out there. I bought worlds of peanuts at the gee-dunk stand for her. She licked our seaplanes for hours, I thought for the salt. But she could've been trying to figure how to bite into the aluminum skin for all I knew. Goats will eat most anything, and from their propensity to lose their kids I knew they are sometimes quite stupid.

I wondered where a goat climbed on Saipan. Our goats at home spent their days at the Lyle place or the Melton place, old abandoned homesteads. They fed in the yards and old fields, and climbed about the old houses. They especially liked the Melton place because it had a two story frame house on it. They went upstairs and out a window onto the porch roof, steep and wood-shingled. Next to this there was an addition to the house with a metal roof.

Carl and I often had to get the goats off the roof so we could all go back to our place after dark. We chased them off the wooden roof onto the metal roof where they slipped off onto the ground. Their hoofs clung to mountains, rocks, and wooden shingles, but smooth metal defeated them.

One night the goats were gone two nights in a row. Sure enough, I found our goats at the old Melton place, and more. Another herd of goats with about a dozen large shaggy- haired billy goats were in the old house with ours. I tried to run them out of the house, but they ran up the stairs on me. I started up the stairs, yelling at them, when they decided to run down all at once. I couldn't get out of the stairwell fast enough, so I ducked down on the stairs, huddled in a ball as the goats clattered past me to the ground. I wanted the billy goats' horns to go over my head. There wasn't enough room for me and their wide horns in that stairway, but somehow we all got out of there without further mishap.

When we got to the bridge across the bayou on the way home, the other goats wouldn't go on it. Our goats were accustomed to crossing the bridge, so it was an easy way to separate our herd from the other. A few months later when our goats had kids, we saw that many of them were shaggy haired.

In Farmdale we had no ice and no electricity. When we butchered an animal we had to sell most of it because we had no way to keep it other than with salt. Pork salt-cured well, but salt wasn't a good method for beef or kid. I developed a taste for goat meat early.

All my goats, Florida and Saipan, were meat goats. I always enjoyed eating goat meat, especially cooked over a wood fire. But I wasn't hungry on Saipan, the goat was. And I had seen enough of killing to last me a long time.

GETTING TO
GO HOME

The military services let us go home from World War II on the basis of a point system. Generally the older fellows like Pop Randall, Tuck, and me, had enough points to go home when the system was announced. Finding a berth on a ship or a plane to get home was another matter.

Scuttlebutt, the Navy grapevine telegraph, had it that VH-3 would fly back to Kaneohe, Hawaii. We would fly Air-Sea Rescue until all the victorious warriors went through on their way home, then take the squadron back to California and decommission it. I tended to believe the scuttlebutt.

Tuck would have none of it — he wanted to use his points immediately and go home at his first opportunity. He said, "Kennedy tried to talk me into staying in and maybe going regular Navy. It sounds like recruit talk to me!"

Remembering the recruiter outlining a Gator Squadron that never came to pass, I understood Tuck's adamant reluctance to be persuaded not to take his points. But I didn't take mine at the time he did. I wanted to fly home, not sail aboard some ship I didn't command.

Official word finally confirmed the scuttlebutt. On October 11, 1945, Crew 5 left Saipan for Eniwetok, Majuro, Johnston Island, and finally to Kaneohe, Hawaii. We left Tuck behind scheduled for troop ship transport; Eddie Meyer was our co-pilot in his place.

Post-war duty was a lot slower. We enjoyed our leisure going from Kaneohe to Honolulu. We went by bus over the Pali, the volcanic cliffs that separated Kaneohe from Waikiki beach. We noticed that all the buses had both corners of their back section as well as both front fenders bashed in terrifically. The old bus belabored itself up the steep grades and around hairpin turns at a slow crawl, grunting, groaning, and spouting steam all the way. About twice on a climb, the Kanaka (native) driver kept going until the bus engine quit. Then he applied the brakes, which didn't hold, and he cocked the front wheels so the bus backed against the cliff with a crunch!!! Crunch!!! Crunch!!! When the engine cooled off, he started up and tried again. The Pali made a much steeper and longer trip than going over the spine of Saipan, but we always made it over and back.

Rather than take the bus one day, I took a jeep to Pearl Harbor, Honolulu, to get Max Hardy, brother of Alton Hardy, the Forest Ranger from home. I brought him back over to Kaneohe to show him through a PBM. Max was an engine man on YP boats at Pearl, accustomed to two or three dials on his yardcraft that supplied ships at the harbor. My PBM had four panels full of instruments and dials, with two more side panels full of switches.

When I sat Max in the PBM engineer's chair, he asked, "Sam, how in the name of heaven can any one man know what all this maze of switches indicates and does? How do y'all keep up with all this?"

I said, "Aw, Max, we ignore 'em a lot of the time."

Which certainly wasn't true, but I was showing off that day, not outright bragging. I thought what Max and I both knew by then about switches and dials was a lot more complicated than the backs of the mules we used to drive through the pine woods.

The decision was made to spend some "morale, welfare, and recreation" funds to hire Sol Kamahali and his family to cater a luau for the whole squadron. They prepared a hog for roasting complete with an apple in its mouth. The night before the feast, they dug a deep hole on the beach, put a number of porous rocks and barbecuing wood in it, and set a wick down in it. At dark, they lit the wick to start the fire. By midnight they had red coals. They put green banana leaves on the hot rocks, then the hog. They piled on more banana leaves, put burlap across the top, and shoveled sand over all of it. Ten hours later the meat was ready.

The day before our luau, an Army Air Corps crew flew into Hickam Field, Honolulu, from the west Pacific, landing right at the time one servicing crew went off and another crew came on duty. No one serviced the airplane.

Early the next morning, the Army Air Corps crew took off for the United States without checking the gas. They ditched in the ocean about 800 miles out. The Navy crew of a nearby Boeing Clipper was diverted to the ditching area. The clipper directed a Navy station ship nearby to the rescue, then departed for California themselves. It did no good for two planes to go down into the drink. Crew 5 was called to search the area for survivors, as not all of the Army Air Corps crew was accounted for. We arrived five hours after the first distress call and set up a thorough search pattern. We knew by then that the Army plane had broken up on ditching.

There were no other survivors. On their way home, too exuberant to pay attention to detail, about half the crew lost their lives. The war was over, but the danger wasn't.

I enjoyed the leftovers of the luau when we got back, but I was shaken by an intense desire to make it all the way home when my turn came.

Our personnel dropped out as they acquired enough points to go home. Irish had been counting the days since the war ended — he was as in love with Sheila as ever, and he wanted to see that baby girl. The day he had enough points, he was checking out.

The squadron Executive Officer by then was Spider McGill. He asked, "Flaherty, why are you in such a hurry to get home?"

Irish said, "I want to be there in time for the birth of my baby." Spider said, "Man, why didn't you tell me that? We could've waived some points and gotten you out earlier. I'll see what I can do right away. When's your baby due?"

With an absolutely straight face, Irish said, "Nine months after I hit the front door."

VH-4 was decommissioned and combined with VH-3 because so many personnel had gone home. We lived in a period of flux. Scuttlebutt was running rampant about where any of us would be next. We tried to organize our shops and turn in all our excess gear, but Base Supply wouldn't take it. We had beau coup tools left over from previous squadrons at Kaneohe, so every Patrol Plane Commander got a 50 calibre shell box full of tools to keep on our planes.

In the midst of all this confused frenzy, Tuck called up on the telephone. He was at Pearl Harbor. I thought he was long gone to Kentucky. It was January, 1946. What on earth was he still doing here? He had difficulty getting transport out of Marpi Point, Saipan, because priority passengers continually bumped him off the schedule. Finally he was put on a ship, smaller than all the others, that had left without him on board. Smaller meant slower. It was so slow that he'd just landed at Pearl. Now he was in another pool, again waiting for transportation to the U.S.

Tuck had sidestepped the "recruit talk," but he hadn't entirely escaped the Navy way. Was he ever mad. All the time we'd been together I had never seen him like this. Fortunately for the good of Pearl Harbor, Tuck eventually got home too.

CALIFORNIA, HERE WE COME

Scuttlebutt was confirmed in February, 1946 — VH-3 was ordered to Alameda, California, for decommissioning. We scurried about to get all the planes and crews together for the flight. HedRon maintenance inspected Crew 5's PBM #59089 two days before we were to takeoff and determined it wasn't airworthy. They pulled it off the line and gave us PBM #59297. It hadn't been used in VH-3 so its JATO wasn't rewired to be efficient on takeoff. It flew clumsy, "laggy," and slow. And sure enough, old #59297 was in worse shape.

We found a rupture in the skin of the hull, a repair that by regulations should go to Overhaul & Repair for repair. Instead of reporting it and enduring delay, we fixed it ourselves. We cut a patch out of some sheet aluminum and drilled holes in it for rivets. We tapped explosive rivets into the holes, held the rivet gun against them and pulled the trigger. The heat from the gun set off a charge in each rivet that expanded the inside adhering the patch onto the hull.

We had used explosive rivets on Johnston Island when a piece of 2x4 lumber knocked a hole in one of our wing floats. It was legal there and then, but not at a Naval Air Station with a HedRon maintenance unit attached to it. So we covered the whole patch with paralketone in order to hide it from the inspectors.

The night before we left, Lutz moonlight-requisitioned three gallons of floor wax out of the cleaning supplies locker at his barracks. When the plane was turned over to us at 1400 hours for loading, our crew waxed the plane, nose to tail, bow to stern, and wing tip to wing tip. They considered the paint was rough, so if the plane were waxed it would slice through the air with less burble and drag, more smoothly—*faster!*

The temporary patch on the hull skin satisfied us, but there was a reason it wouldn't have passed inspection. We could have gone down in the ocean between Hawaii and California — there was a lot of open ocean to traverse, and our plane was not in ideal shape even without the rupture in the hull. On impact, the temporary patch would've given way and let us sink. If we ditched and survived, our tails would be in a crack. Somehow, that didn't faze us one bit.

We went over the side and took off at 1800 hours. We flew in clouds all night, hitting all our navigation points — station ships with radio beacons and communications. At daylight the next morning, we came out of the clouds 100 miles out of Alameda into clear sky and sunshine. Peterson, the Californian said, "Look at the bright sunshine California welcomes us home with!"

We landed at 0900 on March 8, 1946. The last of Crew 5 of the Willie-7 were out of the U.S. ten months and 17 days.

It seemed a lot longer.

The Rewards
of Homecoming

Mary Lona was visiting her brother Paul in Yuba City, California, 130 miles northeast of San Francisco. In Alameda, I waited in a long line until the third schedule had departed before getting on a Greyhound bus. It slowly chugged up to my newlywed wife. Flying across the Pacific had been a whole lot faster. And on this trip, anything would have felt slow.

In Yuba City we bought our first car, a 1937 Dodge we immediately dubbed "Green Hornet" after the popular radio and comic book character. I had all I wanted of lines and delays and riding rather than driving myself. Mary Lona and I found a transient efficiency apartment in a Quonset hut back on the base. With her there, it was the prettiest place I'd ever lived.

The Navy Cross followed me for some time and caught up with VH-3 at Alameda. Admiral W. F. Halsey, Commander of the U.S. Pacific Fleet, had presented the Navy Cross by letter to me in the field. His citation read:

> "For extraordinary heroism while serving as Plane Commander in the successful rescue on 25 July 1945, of three survivors in enemy home waters. Conducting a search of the Inland Sea of Japan which he persisted in, after his escort was forced to leave, he located, landed and picked up a fighter pilot in spite of anti-aircraft fire from shore. Retiring when darkness precluded further search, he had just reached the open sea when he sighted two more pilots two miles southwest of Shikoku. Exhibiting great skill and courage, he successfully landed by moonlight in eight foot swells, brought the two pilots aboard and returned all hands safely to base. His courage, skill and disregard for his personal safety were at all times in keeping with the highest traditions of the United States Naval Service."

Capt. McDade, the Wing Commander of Fleet Air Alameda, presented the Navy Cross medal and ribbon to me in a ceremony with Mary Lona there. The Citation, signed for the President by Secretary of the Navy James Forrestal, read:

> "For extraordinary heroism as Commander of a Rescue Plane in Rescue Squadron Three during operations against enemy Japanese forces in the vicinity of the Japanese Homeland on July 25, 1945. Persisting in a search for two

downed aviators in the Inland Sea of Japan after his escort was forced to leave him, Lieutenant (then Lieutenant Junior Grade,) Davis located and rescued a fighter pilot in the face of anti-aircraft fire from enemy shore batteries. While returning to his base, he sighted two more downed pilots and, executing a skillful landing by moonlight in a rough sea, took them aboard and returned the three airmen safe to base. His superb airmanship and courageous devotion to duty reflect the highest credit upon Lieutenant Davis and the United States Naval Service."

ALL OVER
BUT THE PAPERWORK

O ur three weeks in Alameda were a dream vacation. Mary Lona's nursing school roommate Yvonne Wendell was stationed at the Army hospital in Oakland. We took her and our Navy friends to check out San Francisco every night, tasting savory dishes in Bay area cafes and freezing ourselves almost to numbness. I had been in the tropics all year and had only whites or light weight khaki uniforms to wear. One night my VH-3 C.O. Cdr. R. H. Greer said that when a man freezes to death he appears to laugh, and things were getting awfully funny going up and down San Francisco's hills at 2300 hours.

Three of us remained in VH-3 to finish decommissioning: Greer, Yeoman Peterson who typed well, and me, the Executive Officer by this time. I'd talked to so many Execs over the years, one mild scrape after another, that they figured I should know the drill by then. We finished up the paperwork, of course, but more important to us was writing the last part of the history of VH-3. We boxed up the squadron records and shipped them in a wooden crate to the Navy Department in Washington, D.C.

We three detached ourselves. Peterson took 30 days leave and went home. Greer took 30 days leave and went to duty in Fleet Air Alameda. I took 30 days leave and went to duty in Fleet Air Atlantic in Bermuda. The memory of an exciting tour of duty with the world's most superior men lingers on. The greatest of these was Crew 5 of the Willie-7.

HOMEWARD BOUND

The day we decommissioned VH-3, Mary Lona and I left Alameda in our new old 1937 Dodge, the Green Hornet. I drove that first day and night down the California coast to visit Mary Lona's brother Ernest in Pasadena. He was no longer the younger brother threatening to unravel my suit of his sister with high-jinks.

During the day it was a most beautiful drive along the ocean beaches with the sea lions poking their heads above the water in secluded coves. The Green Hornet carried us along in style, at least until late in the night when the generator quit charging the battery. We got into Pasadena where Ernest lived before the battery gave out, but we had to park the car pointing downhill so we could start it the next day.

We slept a little, then set out to find a garage. It was Sunday. Nothing was open. Finally I found one place where a man had no mechanic on duty but did have some generator brushes. Of course the brushes I could buy weren't the right size, so I bought the larger set to shave down the carbons to fit. I took out the squadron "issued" tools from my squadron "issued" .50 calibre shell box and got to work. I made them fit, the generator worked, and we went back to sleep.

We left about dark that day. Just outside Pasadena there was enough light available for me to drive with the parking lights on to build up the battery. The Highway Patrol stopped me.

The California trooper asked for my driver's license. Without hesitation I pulled out my Navy driver's license from Saipan.

"Commander Davis, don't you have a license from your state?"

"No sir, not since 1942. Florida men returning from overseas could write in and get one, and I've done that. But the license hasn't reached me yet."

"Son, why didn't you get a California driver's license already?"

Uh oh, I hadn't figured on that question. I hadn't figured on getting stopped by the Highway Patrol either. I led the trooper to believe that I'd just bought the car on Saturday in Yuba City and could stop on Monday at a courthouse to get an American Driver's License.

He must have felt pity for my wife being married to someone so dumb. He said, "Go ahead, but run with your headlights on."

I did. We stopped to check into a motel in a little town just before you go across the mountains, but they had no heat. Mary Lona and I had been cold our entire time in California. We knew it was warm in the desert across the mountains. We drove on instead.

I ran into patches of fog as we climbed the slopes. Then the patches connected to each other and thickened. Soon I felt as if I could land a PBM in it. I stopped to turn around and head back toward the coast. To find the edges of the road there, I had to get out of the car and feel where the pavement and the shoulder were so I could safely turn around.

We got back down out of the fog, found the motel again, and rented a cold room for the night. To sleep as warm as possible we put all the cover we could find and all of our clothes on the bed, then crawled in. That night we found that a newly married couple who had been separated by an ocean and a continent for ten months didn't have much problem trying to stay warm.

*Above: Remnant of VH-3; many had already gone home when
Rear Admiral Harold M. Martin presented the Navy unit citation.*

Below: Palmyra, a tropical stop on the way home.

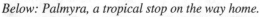

Left: Sam and Willie on Johnston Island   Right: Sam and pet on Saipan

Above: Out for a drive on Saipan
The front seat passenger is Muddy Waters.

*Above: Wing Commander, Captain McDade, presents the
Navy Cross to Sam at Alameda.
Below: Also present at the ceremony;
L to r: R.H. Greer, Sam Davis, Mary Lona Davis,
Kenny Lee, Bob Kidd, and G.W. Carter*

"Admiral" Forgy Davis

CROSS COUNTRY

The next morning Mary Lona and I crossed the mountains into the desert, stopped the car, and lay on the grass beside the road like two alligators alongside the Tamiami Trail in the Florida Everglades. We soon warmed up and travelled on.

We stopped in Globe, Arizona, to visit Great Aunt Lona for whom my mother-in-law was named. We travelled along a mountain road in Arizona where there was snow on the ground — a sight as memorable as the Grand Canyon for two kids from Florida and South Texas. We stopped at Carlsbad Caverns, but the bats were in their Mexico home. We ate a country meal at Aunt Sue's ranch at the junction of the Frio, Atocosa, and Nueces Rivers near Calliham, Texas.

In early April we reached my mother-in-law's farm outside Corpus. One of the first things I did was break out the heavier green and blue uniforms I had stored at Mrs. Forgy's home — I'd been cold since I last left Kaneohe.

We spent three weeks visiting and renewing friendships around Odem, Corpus, and the Naval Air Station at Flour Bluff. My first visit on base, I found people more than surprised to see me, downright startled. After a look of disbelief, my Corpus friends got excited, pumping my hand and saying how glad they were to see me. The experience was repeated everywhere, and I finally had the presence of mind to ask just what was going on.

The Corpus Christi Caller Times had interviewed Mary Lona when the Navy Cross was awarded in the field. Shortly after the interview, she left for California to meet me. The story ran long enough that the newspaper editors cut off the last paragraphs. The result was a story that I had died rescuing the others, and no one was left in Corpus to refute it.

As with Mark Twain, the news of my demise was greatly exaggerated.

Mary Lona and I drove East to Panama City where my people now lived. Daddy was running Davis Trailer Park beside their house in town, and Mama was teaching school. Their lawsuit against the federal government hadn't been settled yet.

Daddy was rounding up his cattle to sell them all. With none of us children at home anymore, it was difficult at his age to tend cattle in three counties. Shortly before I arrived, Daddy got a special permit from the Air Force to go to Tyndall Field to round up some strays after these four war years. He was out there the day the Panama City News Herald printed the New Orleans Navy District news release of our Navy Cross presentation at Alameda.

When Daddy returned to the guard house to check out of the base, the officer asked if he had seen the Panama City paper that day.

Daddy thought the officer was daft — it was obvious with a truck and cattle what Daddy had been doing instead of reading the newspaper. He said, "No, I've been in the woods all day at our old home place."

The officer said, "Here, Mr. Davis, you may be interested in this."

And so my Daddy found out that the US Navy didn't think his boy was a damn fool, that I hadn't crossed his thin line.

One of the first things on my agenda was go to the local oyster bar for boiled shrimp and oysters on the half shell. Mary Lona loved the shrimp and ate the oysters just to be nice to me. When she got nauseated later, she blamed it on the oysters (not the shrimp). Strangely the nausea persisted, especially in the early mornings. She was green around the gills the day she met my sister Eloise, and they seemed to circle each other like wary cats.

Clyde Spann had become an Aviation Machinist Mate in the Navy. He was out of the Navy in 1946 and attending school on the G.I. Bill in his home town of Slocomb, Alabama, when I caught up with him. George Toepher had come out of retirement and served an additional six years of active duty in the war at his old rank of Commander. I thought with his learning and experience they would promote him, but in the Navy, once retired never promoted. Clyde and I called him "Captain" anyway.

I thought I'd go off on my own to see the James girl who had been so disgusted about my draft deferment in 1941. When she saw my uniform and my medals she might think better of me. The war and the military bases had changed things besides Farmdale. I seemed to have trouble orienting myself in Panama City that day. I drove round and round, and finally located where I'd seen the pretty brunette at her family's laundry five years before.

James' Cleaners was gone.

ADMIRAL FORGY DAVIS

Mary Lona and I headed for Norfolk, Virginia, for my duty in Naval Air Atlantic. The Navy was in a personnel turmoil, so we were two weeks in Norfolk awaiting placement in a PBM squadron overseas. The first week we rented a room in the home of Mrs. Little. The second week we rented a room from Mrs. Bigger. Both landladies lived in the community of Oceanview, just outside the east gate of the Norfolk Naval Air Station on the road along the Chesapeake Bay shore toward Virginia Beach.

In the second week, I was assigned to VPB-205 in Bermuda, to fly heavier-than-air craft on anti-submarine bombing patrol. I had three days to square things away at the base, get Mary Lona settled with Mrs. Bigger, and store the Green Hornet in a garage. I was told that the military would fly Mary Lona as a dependent to Baltimore on Naval Air Transport Service (NATS) and then out to Bermuda by British Overseas Airways Corporation (BOAC). I should buy tickets from BOAC in Bermuda because it was cheaper. It would take about three weeks to get her passage.

I called Mary Lona at Mrs. Bigger's and told her to call BOAC to make a reservation right away. I didn't want it to be more than three weeks before I saw her again. I said I'd buy the ticket in Bermuda and send it to her. Then I boarded my flight.

On May 16, 1946, I flew out to Bermuda, 750 miles east of Norfolk, as a passenger. In all my 3,473.3 hours in the air I was the chief pilot except for 35 hours of cadet time. The pilot of this flight was doing some kind of taxiing out, revving up, and turning about I was not accustomed to.

Pilots never seem to be satisfied with another pilot's flying technique, and I was no exception that day. As far as I'm concerned, the only seat worth sitting in is the chief pilot's seat. Behind the chief pilot's seat, the others are all alike.

In five and a half hours we landed in Bermuda. The next day, May 17th, I had a familiarization flight in Bermuda. On May 18th, I was assigned a crew and flew a hop to Norfolk.

When I called Mary Lona in Norfolk, Mrs. Bigger said she had packed up and left for Baltimore about this same time yesterday. NATS told me they had no record of Mary Lona flying to Baltimore with them.

I couldn't imagine what transpired. All I could do was spend the night in Norfolk. The next morning we loaded up for the trip back to Bermuda. I hadn't heard a thing about Mary Lona. The people at NATS said that BOAC ferried passengers by ship to Baltimore, so I determined to check on her whereabouts at the BOAC office when I reached Bermuda.

I landed at 1600 hours on May 19th, turned over the paperwork to the co-pilots to close out our flight, and boarded the fifty foot motor launch at the dock for its regular trip to Hamilton.

Just as the launch came along the dock at Hamilton, everyone's attention was drawn to the BOAC Boeing Clipper making a landing. The pilot smoothed it on pretty well, but did get a small bounce out of the water once before settling in the bay. I said, "I hope they do better than that when they have Mrs. Davis aboard."

I finally arrived at the BOAC office in Hamilton. While I waited my turn at the desk, I saw passengers from the Clipper strolling into the lounge. And there was Mary Lona!

In over 50 years of marriage I learned to expect the unexpected from Mary Lona. It began that day. We waited for two hours together for the launch to our Navy base at King's Point. I found out that she had called the BOAC office in Norfolk as I instructed. They told her she could fly out anytime with them. She retorted, "Well, my husband said there would be a waiting period, and then I'd have to get on NATS to go to Baltimore."

BOAC said, "No, Mrs. Davis, you can leave here Tuesday night on our ship, go up the Chesapeake Bay to Baltimore, and board our Clipper to Bermuda on Wednesday morning."

She said, "My husband said it's cheaper for him to buy the ticket in Bermuda and not have to pay U.S. taxes on it."

"Yes, Mrs. Davis, he can do that. But you can purchase the ticket on the ship. It covers the ship to Baltimore and the plane to Bermuda. It will be less expensive than if he bought it in Bermuda and sent the ticket to you."

So Mary Lona had packed her bag, paid Mrs. Bigger for the room, called a taxi, and boarded the ship. That was that! Wasn't I glad to see her?

Of course I was glad to see her. Delighted! I also sort of envied her the seaplane flight on one of the pre-World War II Boeing Clippers that was the ultimate in passenger service over both oceans.

Mary Lona was so excited she spent far into the night telling me how she fared on this adventure. Her ship up the Chesapeake Bay was in fog. They blew the fog horn intermittently all night, and other ships answered hers in turn. She said when the fog horn blew, it awakened the man in the next cabin who cursed vehemently each time. She, on the other hand, found the sound romantic.

My flight in the PBM had been uneventful, as I doglegged to the south of my course to remain in clear air. Mary Lona's Clipper flew north of my flight, bouncing and tumbling in terrific rain. She could look up the companionway to the pilot's seat and see him working the rudders and the wheel as they rode over the up and down currents. Scared at first, she saw the crew was calm, and then she was no longer frightened. I heard much about the perfect manners of the British steward on the Clipper that trip.

I also had a problem. I hadn't had time to apply for housing. There was no clearance for her to come to Bermuda. It was already late when we reached King's Point, so she bunked happily with me at the Bachelor Officers Quarters and ate at the BOQ mess. The next morning I went around to the necessary officials on the base about her.

Everywhere I went May 20th for clearance for Mary Lona, they asked me, "When does she want to come?"

"Well, you see, she's - uh - already here." They all asked how she got to Bermuda without permission.

I grinned every time and said, "In this family she considers her rank to be that of a Fleet Admiral. You ask her."

INDEPENDENCE DAY
ON BRITISH SOIL

M y squadron in Bermuda had been lax on standard procedure, so when I was made gunnery officer I had to look up all the regulations on gunnery and safety to write up a set of squadron orders to cover all our procedures. Warrant Officer M. D. Kemper, gunnery officer of the Bermuda Naval Station, helped greatly in this endeavor. Together we found numerous supplies of ammunition were stockpiled during the war, and it was now assigned to VPB-205 to get rid of it. By regulation, most of the ammo and pyrotechnics were too old to be used safely unless they passed a firing test. We'd have to dump what couldn't pass.

It was early July, 1946. Kemper and I gave the orders to our respective gunnery chiefs to test-fire the ammo. The Commanding Officer of the Naval Station, Adm. G. R. Henderson, saw star shell flares go up as he returned to the island from a 4th of July party. When he drove to the sea ramp to investigate, the chief told him they were officially test-firing outdated ammo on my order.

The Admiral wasn't satisfied with the chief's explanation. He ordered them to quit for the night and wait for Mr. Davis's orders the next day.

Early the morning of July 5th, Squadron Chief Jones reported all this to me. We quickly reviewed the Naval regulation codes about testing and dumping ammo. Jones told me they had test-fired a batch of star shells used for warning signals and rescue locations. It was their opinion these had failed the test and had to be disposed of by firing them that night, on my order.

I called Kemper. His men reported the same.

About 0900, the Admiral's Aide called our C.O., Cdr N. K. Brady. He, Kemper, Jones, and I were to be in the Admiral's office at 1000 for a conference. All of us sent a sailor in a jeep to our quarters for clean shirts and jackets. Brady told the sailor to be sure he returned with a jacket with my Navy Cross ribbon on it. I would be the spokesman.

The meeting with the Admiral started off very brisk and military. I tried to answer questions as if we all knew verbatim the Navy regs on handling ammunition. Finally the Admiral asked if I or my chief could explain what really happened.

I thought I detected a slight indication of pity or amusement in the Admiral's voice. I said, "Admiral Henderson, we issued the orders to the men to test-fire and dump the ammo and pyrotechnics as appropriate to Naval Regulations. We specifically let our two Gunnery Chiefs perform this task on their own initiative in compliance with the recent 'Al Nav' on this subject, knowing full well the Chiefs knew the Naval Regulations concerning testing and dumping ammo. I think that Chief Jones, having scheduled the test firing of the star shells on 4th of July night, would indicate unquestionable patriotism, even though we are on a British island."

It was the best I could do with my backwoods demeanor and philosophy showing.

The Admiral's aide turned to hide his smile. The Admiral almost laughed out loud. We left without a reprimand or a tongue lashing. We never found out if the Navy Cross ribbon had anything to do with it.

VOLUNTEERED

July 5, 1946 was a long day. The station heard an emergency call on the 500 kilocycle radio band from a Russian merchant ship. They needed serum for gangrene. One of their seaman was injured in a tropical storm in the Atlantic about halfway from Bermuda to the Azores off Portugal to the west. We were the nearest station to their ship that had the serum and the means of getting it to them.

Aerology plotted the storm as having already passed by the Russian ship, so I, with the reputation of being one who could fly the hangar doors, was volunteered for this duty. I had Bill Leary and his bragging about VH-3 to thank for this, if not the Navy Cross.

We flew east and doglegged to the north, then turned down southward to go through the edge of the storm. The ship was in a clear area, but the seas remained too rough for a seaplane landing. The serum was packaged to withstand dropping on the deck of the ship. We trailed out a line with the serum package tied in the middle of it. Passing over the ship, we dropped the package on the deck into waiting hands that waved back in thanks.

When the Russian ship put into Bermuda three days later, I learned that the seaman lived. I had flown another kind of Air-Sea Rescue.

SHOWTIME

Bermuda was a popular place to visit. We had the composer of "God Bless America," Irving Berlin, visit one of our beach parties. Mary Lona and I had tea with Thomas Moore, the British poet, at the house of his islander friend Mrs. Rigby. British Royalty put all their subjects into a dither when they stopped in port. But the most exciting guest of the Bermuda Naval Station for me was the President of the United States of America.

President Harry S. Truman started on a trip down the Potomac River and north up the coast of the USA. However, as usual, the ocean had its own ideas. Bad weather set in, so the Presidential yacht Williamsburg put into Bermuda instead of going north.

For a few days the press had no idea where President Truman was. It was my impression he was tickled at that.

We always had VIPs visiting from Washington, D.C. Whether the visits were official or not, they were still treated with the greatest courtesy. This visit we flew the President's entourage of publicists, cronies, and "yes men" on a sight-seeing tour of the islands. We just happened to show off our Navy planes at the same time.

Our station had already set up a flight demonstration and other festivities to begin the next day to celebrate Navy Day. I was scheduled to demonstrate one of two JATO takeoffs, to show the application of jet technology to seaplanes in short takeoff waters.

For my demonstration on Navy Day, I hand-picked a skeleton crew to make my plane a lot lighter for climbing. I purposely flew a load of the President's entourage in my plane on the sight-seeing tour until we had burned all but 800 gallons of its gasoline supply. When we landed, I took care that no one gassed her up again, detailing Chief Anderson to park the plane and lock it after it was pre-flight-checked for the next day.

The Navy Day festivities began with a parade for Mr. Truman and his group as well as several officers and men from the British Naval Base and invited guests from Bermuda. At 1400 hours, Lt. Frank Pawella and I took our planes out to demonstrate seaplane flying and JATO takeoff from the waters of Great Sound. Frank took off first using the regular, recommended, safe procedure.

I and my crew, on the other hand, held our plane on the water until we reached flying speed, then fired all four JATO bottle rockets. As light as my plane was, she shot up off the water with her nose pointed skyward like a homesick angel. We gained 900 feet in 12 seconds; the normal rate of climb of a PBM was 500 feet per minute. A photographer took pictures constantly from the crash boat near the seadrome with an excellent view of our takeoff.

Somehow the Naval Station got these into the Bermuda newspaper with a write-up of Navy Day 1946. Those who were ignorant of seaplane flying thought my takeoff was spectacular. Some who knew about seaplanes thought it was a dangerous maneuver. They were both right. I had taken a calculated risk to play to our audience. It was fun, a show, an entertainment for our guests. It was not routine procedure.

NEVER A
DULL DAY

In November, I flew my assigned PBM-5 to Norfolk with the body of a Navy man killed on his motorbike in Bermuda. I was assigned to fly his casket in a wooden shipping box for train shipment from Virginia to his home in Alabama. It was a chore to load the box into the rear doors of my PBM and jockey it into place under the deck turret.

Bad weather was brewing in Norfolk that day when we left Bermuda, but it was expected to get better. Of course the weather worsened instead. At 200 miles out we called to find out the wind at Norfolk; it was 40 knots. I decided to call Philadelphia where there was a seadrome at an old Naval aircraft factory.

Yes, the wind was better, 8 knots. No, permission to divert to Philadelphia was denied due to the nature of our cargo. By the time we entered the pattern for landing in Willoughby Bay, Virginia, the north wind was at 45 knots, gusting to 52 knots. We landed at the lee side of Willoughby Spit because the water was not so rough there. I called the station to suggest that beaching the PBM in this wind was hazardous. May we anchor near the shore and wait for better weather to unload the casket onto a launch?

The Wing Commander sent a message asking the pilot to make the ramp buoy. The wind was blowing straight onto the ramp, so I came barreling in with excess taxiing speed downwind and swung the plane completely around at the buoy, adjusting the throttles to equal the wind drift. When I had my bow door dead on the head right at the buoy, I reported "buoy made" to the Wing control.

No one at Norfolk that day seemed willing to wait out the weather for calmer winds. The beaching crew began floating wheels out to attach them onto the plane's hull and pull us ashore. They had a hard time with the wind, the waves, and the cold. In the melee, a large wave slapped the beaching gear up against my plane and pierced a hole in the side of the hull.

We started the electric pump, but the water came in faster than we could pump it out. We tried to apply the temporary hull patches, but the hole was in an area too inaccessible for those. I called for a fire truck to come out, put a suction hose in our plane, and pump it out. The men with the fire truck refused to try.

I told our crew to close all the watertight doors between the compartments. That's when we found out the watertight doors weren't.

We all got wet, cold, and meaner by the minute. Finally, we got the beaching gear main wheels mounted, but the plane was pitching so that we couldn't get the tail gear attached. By that time water had floated our cargo up and lodged it against the bottom of the deck turret.

We could see where the water rose several inches up on the side of the casket shipping box. When I saw what turned out to be the stain of a broken sea die marker in the water, I thought at the time that blood was oozing out of the box.

After hours of trying to get ashore, I ended up in the turret with the outside hatch open, shouting my commands up there into the wind. I was almost frantic to get the hole in my seaplane out of the water. I was up there when the funeral home hearse drove up to the crowd of helpers, bosses, and spectators that had gathered around us.

This neatly dressed man got out of the hearse and yelled to me that he didn't want to get salt water from the cargo on the carpets of his hearse. Had it gotten wet? Something in me snapped. I boiled over like an overheated tea kettle, because I hadn't seen anything or anyone that wasn't wet in a long time. In an instant I bellowed, "Hell yes! It's floated in six feet of salt water for hours!"

Finally, the fire truck crew came out and suction-pumped all the water from all the compartments of the plane. If they had done that when I first called for it, we wouldn't have been in the rotten shape we were by the time they arrived.

I never learned why the fire truck crew delayed, and I never knew why Norfolk had no jack capability to lift the tail of my plane high enough to attach the tail beaching wheels. Someone on shore now decided they would lift my plane with a mobile crane.

The beaching crew put a cable around the tail assembly behind the rearmost part of the plane's keel. They shored up the cable with 2x6s and began lifting. The cable tightened.

The crane groaned as more pressure was needed. The tail began to lift when ... WHAMMO!! A 2x6 timber split asunder. It was the one 12 foot long 2x6 that was supposed to spread the cable so it didn't cut into the skin of my plane.

When this timber snapped, the cable whipped right into the skin of the tail assembly, cutting ribs and skin for about 12 inches on each side. With the hole in the hull, hours of flooding, and the wrecked tail assembly, all 124 electrical dynamometers below the flight deck of this PBM-5 were ruined. The plane didn't sink, but it was destroyed none the less.

It was 2330 hours before we squared the plane away so that we could unload the cargo. By then, the funeral hearse was nowhere to be found. We found a duty section at the base hospital that sent a truck to get our cargo. I went with the ambulance to the hospital where they opened the shipping box to find it hadn't leaked salt water through to the casket. Through all the havoc and mania, the dead man had rested in peace after all.

LOST AND FOUND

O n December 6, 1946, I was on an instrument training flight that was routine until the weather actually closed in and it became the real thing.

The Bermuda low frequency range station had been unreliably fluctuating. This day it was in its unreliable phase.

My co-pilot, Mark Ingraham, and I found a hole in the clouds at the north end of Bermuda. The Bermuda British Naval Base was on a point south of the ship's channel, about 15 miles from the north tip of the island.

I told him we would come down to 500 feet above the water, take up a heading of 235 degrees, and fly for five minutes in hopes of spotting the British base. When we saw it, we could turn down the ship's channel and follow the channel buoys as guides to the U.S. Naval Station. We'd set her down near our station and wait for the weather to clear to taxi on in. We were in the soup. Neither of us could see the British Station. We dared not go lower than 500 feet, as we could see nothing of ships, buildings, or other aircraft. Five minutes were consumed, then five and half. At six minutes, I said, "Mark, we've missed it, so we'd better climb out and get on the range even though it is unreliable."

Just then, I glimpsed the tower on the tallest building on the British base — only a glimpse. It was unmistakable for its clock face similar to Big Ben on Parliament Building in London.

I wheeled around in a non-gliding split "S." As we lowered slightly, we could see a channel marker in the ship's channel. As we went lower, we saw the next one. We flew from marker to marker this way, on up the seven miles to King's Point where we settled in the water by our own base. Mark took off his headset and said,

"Yeah. I'll fly with you."

I thought maybe the noise of the PBM had drowned Mark out before the engines stopped, and I'd missed some talk preliminary to his comment. To get into the conversation Mark seemed to be having, I asked, "Where?"

He said, "Any damn place you want to go." It was the supreme compliment from one pilot to another, and I knew it.

LONA FRANCES

In the early evening of December 8, 1946, Mary Lona received a message from Mr. Coe, the farmer of her mother's place at Odem, Texas. Mrs. Forgy had been in a terrible car wreck and was almost killed but still alive.

My mother-in-law had become my buddy when she visited us in Bermuda a few months back, and I took the news hard. The shock was greater for Mary Lona; she went into premature labor that day, six weeks before our first baby was due.

At 0200 hours, I called Mary Lona's doctor at the base, Dr. Yon, and he came by with a sedative to try to slow things down. The next day Mary Lona awoke feeling better, and we began to check on many things. I reached Mr. Coe to find that Mrs. Forgy had broken one of every kind of bone in her body.

Everyone was surprised she had survived the wreck. Her mangled jaw would be set in a few days. Her broken leg had already been set, and she seemed okay for now.

We toyed with the idea of going by plane to Corpus on NATS. Dr. Yon warned that the flight could trigger labor, but with this being a first baby, there would be time to set down at a Navy Base with a hospital in time for Mary Lona to be cared for. We scheduled a plane at Kindley Field in Bermuda for 1000 hours December 10th. For the first of many times in her life, this child had plans of her own.

At 0200 hours, Mary Lona went into labor.

I took the Exec's jeep and ran her over to the Base hospital at King's Point.

This was no time to use my American Whizzer motorcycle with the sidecar.

At breakfast five hours later, I took the jeep back to the Exec, Lt. Cdr. Des Galier. I called Kindley Field to cancel our flight. Then I went back to sick bay.

The squadron got a call that morning that a ship was off Bermuda with a seaman whose appendix had ruptured. The Squadron C.O. Brady said, "This is just the time we need Sam, and he's headed for Texas today."

Des Galier spoke up, "No, Sam has Mary Lona in the base hospital in labor."

Brady called Dr. Yon to see if I could be available. Like the distant kinsman he was, Dr. Yon said, "We better keep Sam here to watch the guinea nest."

In fact, Mary Lona had a miserable pregnancy, even being hospitalized for an infected appendix while carrying our baby. Dr. Yon had treated her successfully with loads of antibiotics, the new thing in medicine then. He hadn't had to operate to save Mary Lona's life and risk losing her baby. He'd brought Mary Lona and the baby safely through to this point, and he had our confidence. This was especially important to Mary Lona — as a nurse she did not give her confidence to any doctor lightly.

Brady asked for me to come to the telephone. That was fine with Dr. Yon. When I came on the line, Brady said, "I'm going to get Frank Pawella to fly this hop. Can you brief him on open sea landing?"

The only answer was "Yes Sir." Frank came on the line , and I did the best I could. He was an experienced pilot, having flown many years as an AP like the fabulous Fondren, before becoming a Mustang like "Captain" Toepher. These men could flat fly.

Unfortunately, the seas were quite heavy near the offshore ship. One wave zapped the bow of Frank's seaplane so hard that his clamshell doors over the bomb-sight window broke off. The window broke with the pressure, half filling the bow of the plane with water. The plane didn't sink, however.

The flight surgeon on Frank's plane, Dr. Jock McCurdy, was able to board the ship to care for the seaman. But Frank's plane couldn't fly.

When Des Galier heard about this, he called me again at the Bermuda sick bay. Mary Lona's labor was going pretty well by then, so I went to the operations office where I might be more useful than I was while sitting in the father's waiting room.

My idea was to make a temporary repair by cutting plywood in the ship's shop to fit the bow window and using a couple of sturdy wool Navy blankets for gaskets. Wooden planks could be cut to lengths to jam the plywood in place.

If it worked, they could taxi the plane back in. My idea came from my old VH-3 mindset to taxi anywhere, anytime, if you had to save a plane.

We batted other ideas around until a decision was made to send out a tugboat, which could arrive at the Naval Station the next day, and tow the plane in. I went back to sick bay.

Unfortunately, Mary Lona took the position that our firstborn was more important than Frank Pawella's plane. Funny what ten hours of labor can do to your viewpoint!

Irish and Sheila Flaherty's second daughter was born nine months and three weeks after he got home. Tuck and Evelyn's baby was due in 1947. Mary Lona's and my first baby was born at 1400 hours on December 10, 1946, nine months and two days after I landed in Alameda, California. We named our daughter Lona Frances, after her mother and my Daddy's beloved oldest sister. But mostly that day we named her for her Grandmother Forgy.

THE DAY AFTER

Nothing was easy on December 11, 1946. The legal aspects of registering Lona's birth were complicated by the fact that the hospital was on the grounds of the Bermuda Naval Station, where the U.S. leased but did not own the land. In inimitable British fashion, that was interpreted to mean she was born on British soil and therefore a British subject.

Since her mother and I were U.S. citizens, we wanted to take our baby home to the States. I couldn't make any headway about my child's U.S. citizenship. She was inexorably issued a British birth certificate with King George VI's gold seal. By law she could become a British subject on her 21st birthday automatically if she chose to apply. When we left Bermuda, I would have to register her with the U.S. Consul in Bermuda to bring her through U.S. customs.

The tugboat got to Frank Pawella's plane and prepared to tow it to Bermuda. They hadn't been able to empty the plane of water before they tied a rope and chain to the tail.

The plan was to bring her in tail first, probably because the tail of a PBM is the smallest diameter of its fuselage.

However, when the tug got underway, the tail broke off.

The plane sank irretrievably in the Atlantic.

A Court of Inquiry was formed on the loss of Frank's seaplane. I was on the Court. Then somebody in the Squadron or the Wing discovered nothing had been done about the loss of my seaplane at Norfolk in November.

I was called on to write a report for the squadron to hold a Court of Inquiry on me. Frank Pawella was a member of my Court. Neither of us tried to hang the other one. The Navy never saw fit to hold any money out of our pay for the two seaplanes. December 11, 1946, was not one of the better days in my life.

LEAVING BERMUDA

M ary Lona, Lona Frances, and I spent our first Christmas together in Bermuda. Mrs. Forgy had a setback, but we couldn't move our baby because she was losing weight. If it hadn't been the season of Christian hope, I might not have had any.

In January 1947, the Bermuda Naval Station received a directive from the Navy Department to set up strict accounting procedures and live within its allocated budget. Soon after, the Navy Department sent word that the Reserves who had been on active duty through the war years would be released.

On January 27, 1947, I gave instructions in seaplane night landings to two new pilots on my last hop in the PBM-5. In the next few days, we Reservists closed out our World War II Navy careers.

I took my watch and binoculars as excess Navy issue and had the presence of mind to buy my flight jacket made of leather, silk, and fur.

I flew to Norfolk to be detached. We didn't have a car on Bermuda. The island had severe restrictions of the horsepower allowed in vehicles, so almost everyone rode bicycles and motorcycles.

When I reached Virginia and finished my Navy business, I took our "Green Hornet" car out of storage and drove it to the Naval Air Station at Patuxent River, Maryland. Then I caught a ride on NATS to Kindley Field in Bermuda.

I wasn't the chief pilot anymore.

On February 11, 1947, we bundled up our baby girl and carefully placed her on a pillow in a pasteboard box. Her head was still the size of an orange, and her legs were exactly the same dimensions as my first two fingers. She was too small for a regular baby bassinet. Lona slept through her first airplane flight, in her little box beside us. She breathed her first American air at a United States Naval Air Station — Patuxent.

We drove to Odem, Texas, where Mary Lona promptly took charge. She fired Mrs. Forgy's doctors, hired her own, and started her mother on the road to recovery.

Nursing a six-week-old infant didn't slow down Mary Lona Forgy Davis, the Registered Nurse. When life on the farm settled down a bit, I went in to Corpus to find more old colleagues and friends. Most of them were totally surprised to see me. This time I had an idea about what had happened.

Sure enough, my friends had read a Corpus Christi Caller Times story about my Navy Cross that implied I had not survived going up inside Japan to fetch Yoder, Smith, and Selway. I had a second chance to counter the exaggerated rumors of my demise.

On June 27, 1947, the Secretary of the Navy wrote to me c/o Mrs. M. D. Forgy, Odem, Texas. It was individually typed and signed. It read:

"My dear Lieutenant Davis;

I have addressed this letter to reach you after all the formalities of your separation from active service are completed. I have done so because, without formality but as clearly as I know how to say it, I want the Navy's pride in you, which it is my privilege to express, to reach into your civil life and to remain with you always. You have served in the greatest Navy in the world. It crushed two enemy fleets at once, receiving their surrenders only four months apart. It brought our land-based airpower within bombing range of the enemy, and set our ground armies on the beachheads of final victory. It performed the multitude of tasks necessary to support these military operations. No other Navy at any time has done so much. For your part in these achievements you deserve to be proud as long as you live. The Nation which you served at a time of crisis will remember you with gratitude. The best wishes of the Navy go with you into your future life.

Good luck! Sincerely yours, James Forrestal"

Mr. Secretary, I have followed your advice. I shall be proud of our Navy achievements for as long as I live.

THE UNIVERSITY
OF CORPUS CHRISTI

By the summer of 1947, Mrs. Forgy was still too frail to be left alone. My brother-in-law, Ernest Forgy, and I were taking care of Lona when Mary Lona was with her mother.

Rather than return to Florida and leave everyone in this predicament, I enrolled for the fall semester at the University of Corpus Christi, a new college organized by the Southern Baptist General Convention of Texas.

I registered for math, biology, and public speaking courses I needed that would transfer to Florida. To fill out a full term, I took the introductory Bible course.

I had grown up with rotating Baptist, Methodist, and Church of God preachers and weekly Sunday School in Farmdale, but these Texas Baptists were really thorough about the Holy Bible. By the time fall arrived, the family requirements on Mary Lona eased enough for her to enroll in a college course as well.

We went to Austin for her training school records for her nurse's registration in Texas. She had so many science courses and laboratory classes that U.C.C. classified her as a Junior. Her culminating triumph that semester came when she made a letter grade higher than I did in the Bible course.

THE UNIVERSITY
OF FLORIDA

In the spring of 1948, I had to take Forestry courses that weren't offered at U.C.C. There was no forestry to speak of in South Texas, all those mesquite trees being poor woods. If I had to leave Odem and Corpus for school, I may as well return 1200 miles to Gainesville and pick up my forestry career again at the University of Florida.

I had not given up my desire to be a graduate forester. I believed, with good reason, that the Forestry School at Florida was the best in the nation.

Under Mary Lona's care and supervision, Mrs. Forgy was improving. Lona was growing like a weed. Our second baby was on its way, due the summer of 1948. As it turned out, our precious little girl Mary Dee was born in the nearest hospital at Sinton, Texas, on June 5, 1948.

I was the proud father of two daughters by the time I celebrated my 31st birthday. It wasn't easy, but it was possible for me to leave Texas for the spring semester in Gainesville.

Mary Lona could live on her mother's farm with her family. I could live at the CLO house on my G.I. Bill stipend and send her some of it. My tuition was paid on the G.I. Bill as well. With the help of a grateful nation, I could continue my education and support my family. They would join me for the fall 1948 semester.

When I enrolled again at the University of Florida, all my credits transferred. After some head-scratching, they gave me three hours credit in history for the Bible course.

I went around to see old friends back in Gainesville, too. Buck Battle and Henry Cone from the original "Gator Squadron" enlistments were at the CLO house. Henry kept saying, "Sam, it's so *good* to see you!"

Buck repeated much the same sentiment and just about as often. I finally cottoned on that the Gainesville Sun had run the same story about my demise as had the Corpus and Panama City papers. The relief expressed by Henry and Buck made me feel downright resurrected.

The CLO House was in the same place, and the Forestry School was still full of country boys. But everything else was changed.

Before the war, Florida had 5,000 men on campus. In 1948, I was one of 10,000 men and women enrolled on campus. More students came each semester. By the time I left in 1950, enrollment was much larger.

The Coeds had arrived in my absence, and men were attending the former Florida State College for Women in Tallahassee. The University moved barracks from Camp Blanding at Starke to Gainesville for classrooms, dormitories, and student apartments. Classes were held on the lawns, not so much because of the balmy weather as for the necessary room.

Fortunately for forestry majors, many of our courses were taught in the University's Austin Cary Forest, 2,000 acres of managed woodland on the road from Gainesville to Waldo.

I signed up on the waiting list for married student housing in Florida Veteran's Village, quickly dubbed FlaVet by all of us familiar with military jargon. FlaVet was campus housing put together from one-story surplus government buildings. These had been intended for temporary offices and barracks when they were built, and they looked it. In hindsight, many of the places of the 1940s we had to live in were crummy. But World War II had moved millions of Americans around, sending us to military bases and opening plants so rapidly that nearby housing was swamped with soldiers and workers needing a place to sleep.

During the war, industrial resources were diverted from civilian demands to supply the military war effort. If we had shelter from the rain that was enough, never mind how limited our access to plumbing or how many years we did without kitchen privileges. Mary Lona and I had eaten all the tuna sandwiches and hamburgers we ever wanted to see again during the war.

Housing immediately after the war was still scarce, with the added pressure that veterans were coming back into the housing market. Not just single veterans either. If we weren't married, we got married. If we were married, we had babies.

The Baby Boom was the name given to the increase in live births in the U.S. that began in 1946. It took a few years before the federal government guarantees of mortgages for veterans under the G.I. Bill stimulated sufficient home building to meet the demand. Even with the war over, it seemed as if every American was still on the move.

My journeys from California to Texas to Florida to Virginia to Maryland, back and forth thousands of miles, were not unusual.

Mary Lona and I were typical — she would not stay in Odem, Texas, and I would not return to Farmdale, Florida. It seemed that our lives had gone on hold for the war effort, we had to make up for lost time, and we were never going back to be where we had been before.

The federal government was expecting a return to the hard economic times of the Great Depression.

Women who had so ably supplied the war effort in industry were fired by the millions to make room for returning veterans to take those jobs.

As the war wound down, the federal government contracted with some sociologists to find out what we veterans needed on our return to civilian life. Their results were incorporated into legislation known everywhere as the G.I. Bill. Our two greatest needs were housing and civilian jobs.

It was found that government insurance for veterans' mortgages could make up for the years we had spent in the military services rather than working to save for down payments. We were given preference points for jobs to make up for the years we had not been advancing in civilian careers. And best of all for me, tuition and living stipends were provided if we qualified for further education or training.

I was over 30 years old and back in school. The Forestry School faculty were much the same, but the graduate school filled with veterans who joined the forestry faculties at Florida, Georgia, Alabama, and Auburn Universities over the years. I was going to school with students aged 20 to 40.

We had in common a serious purpose to make the most of our burgeoning opportunities. All of us veterans had seen good men die when we had been spared. We felt obligated to them to make something of ourselves. It was an obligation we also felt to the Nation we had worked so hard to preserve through the years.

MERLIN DIXON

In Dallas Pre-Flight training in 1942, I had met a tall, lanky young man with wavy black hair from Daytona Beach who transferred in from the Royal Canadian Air Force (RCAF). I didn't learn his name, but the memory of him remained. After the war, I became staunch friends with Merlin Dixon at the University of Florida School of Forestry.

In the summer after our first year together on the G.I. Bill, Merlin mentioned a pillow fight to outdo all pillow fights he had been in. After about ten minutes of Merlin describing the pillow fight, I chimed in that I, too, had been in just that sort of thing years ago at the Naval Air Station in Dallas. Merlin asked when I was there. I told him September, 1942.

Merlin said, "So was I. Were you in the first barracks or the second?"

I answered, "The second."

"So was I. Were you on the lower deck or the upper deck?"

"The upper deck." Merlin concluded, "We were in the same pillow fight."

I knew then that the tall lanky Daytona Beach boy from the RCAF was my friend and forestry colleague Merlin Dixon.

The war had changed us both. Thirty-five years later, I took my grandson on our first fishing trip together on Merlin's stretch of the Homosassa Springs River in Florida.

Merlin was still memorable. We two men kept busy baiting the boy's hook and seeing that he could catch the fish as they swam up to our boat in the transparent water. The little boy was entranced by all of it. He returned in great excitement from the trip, face lit up and his proudest moment on his lips. "Mom! Dad! I caught the biggest fish, and I caught more fish than Grandpa and Mr. Dixon, and they're foresters!"

I couldn't have been more proud.

HOME AGAIN
FOR THE FIRST TIME

I knew when I went to work for Alton Hardy and Uncle John that I was getting away from farming. I knew when I went to the University of Florida that I was preparing for a young man's adventure of war. I knew when Crew 5 of the Willie-7 lifted off San Diego bay that I was going as far as possible from my Florida home.

I had my adventure. I flew the finest seaplanes in the world in the greatest conflict of my century. I was awarded the highest commendation of the oldest military service of the most powerful nation on earth. I faced the greatest challenge in the Navy, death at sea. But I didn't face it alone.

The Navy never said Boo nor Turkey to anyone else in Crew 5 of the Willie-7. No other medals, no commendations, not even a nice letter. I suppose it's the Navy way — the court martial would have been mine alone if we had lost our ship. But I didn't like it then, and I don't like it now.

Every man in Crew 5 saved my life and brought us all home.

In the end, that was what I wanted most, to go home. I wanted to be with Mary Lona. I wanted to see my folks. If I couldn't fly my lovely seaplanes, I wanted to tend my sandy pine woods. And I was lucky; I got that chance.

Returning to the campus of the University of Florida was like coming full circle to where I took off on a life of adventure.

I never forgot that I was a Cracker country boy. When I was a lumber company agent, I seemed to be the only one who took off his coat and tie out in the woods, and talked the country language of my childhood to the pulpwood farmers. I also consistently secured more wood for the company's saw mill than the other agents.

I finished my bachelor's degree in forestry and the course work for my master's degree at the University of Florida when the Navy Reserve called me back into active duty. I packed up the notes for my thesis in a briefcase and took off for Kwajalein and Hawaii for the next three years. The thesis notes are still in the briefcase.

My forestry career spanned 43 years. I worked for every State Forester Florida ever had until I retired: Harry Lee Baker; Henry Mahlsberger; Clinton Huxley Coulter; John Bethea; and Harold K. Mikel. I believe my respect and affection for them was reciprocated. Hux Coulter made a special trip to my retirement party, and before he was done with his talk we were both in tears.

However much I respected these men, I repeatedly turned down forestry assignments in the state capital, Tallahassee. I knew I was happiest out in the field in just about everything I ever did. I loved being in on the real action, making as short shrift of paper shuffling as I decently could. I conducted my forestry career much as I had brought all hands and survivors back at night from Japan — with headquarters hundreds of miles away.

Thirty years after I graduated from Bay High School, a woman I hadn't seen since graduation asked in a mildly condescending way just what I had managed to do with myself. She had last seen me as a backwoods country boy determined never to darken a school door again.

Her surprise seemed to deepen with each line of my reply. "You went to college after all? ... You served in the Navy? ... You graduated from the University at Gainesville? ... You teach forestry courses now?"

I didn't have the heart to mention the Navy Cross or graduate school.

Now I go to family reunions as a Grandpa Davis in my own right. Recently I listened to a young relative striving to leave the town where his grandfather's name is on a town-square building, for riches elsewhere. I told him, "You know, my lifetime dream, my ultimate goal, was to reach a utopia in town, in a bigger place. I made it to Panama City, then Gainesville, then out of Florida altogether. I travelled the world in war and in peace. I made it, and finally I recognized the utopia. I returned to my native country."

I came back for the serenity, peace, and solitude I took for granted so long ago.

I came back from as far away as I could go, from an adventure that would never be equalled in my lifetime. Even with all the changes wrought by war, I came to the place from whence I began and knew it for the first time.

Above:
Frank Pawela's crippled seaplane in the Atlantic near Bermuda
Below:
Sam and crew flew President Harry S. Truman's press party
around Bermuda.

Above: Mary Lona and Mrs. Rigby, our hostess for tea with Thomas Moore, near our rented home, "High Ferry"

Above left: Ocean front vacation home where Irving Berlin stayed
Above right: Mary Lona and Lona Frances

Above: JATO Take-off demonstration for President Truman's visit to Bermuda, Navy Day, 1946

All Nellie's Children:
Above left; Jim Davis, Chief Engineer, Merchant Marine
Above right; Carl Davis, Chief Engineman, U.S. Coast Guard

Above left; Eloise D. Cain,
Above right; Sam Davis, Cadet at Georgia pre-flight school

PBM over Bermuda

Chapter Notes
pg.   note

Born on the Florida Frontier

8   1   "that wasn't yet Bay County" Womack, Marlene. 1994. *Along the Bay, a pictorial history of Bay County*. Norfolk, VA: Pictorial Heritage Publishing Co., pp. 65, 90.

8   2   "the first charter ... to a state university" Georgia Historical Society marker at Bay Street near the Chamber of Commerce, Savannah, Georgia. The complete text is in Scruggs, Carroll Proctor (compiler). 1973. *Georgia Historical Markers*. Helen, GA: Bay Tree Grove. p. 90.

9   3   "Iola" *Golden Anniversary Celebration, Gulf County, Florida*. June 6-14, 1975. Chattanooga, TN: Great American Publishing Company, p. 31.

9   4   "the Samuel Pasco Davis family" Eleanor Russell and Samuel Pasco Davis were married March 21, 1910, at Chason, Florida.

9   5   "Farmdale" Bell, Harold G. 1961. *Glimpses of the Panhandle*. Chicago: Adams Press, pp. 5, 43. Hutchison, Ira Augustus. 1951-1954. *Some Who Passed This Way*. Privately published from stories written for a Panama City weekly paper between November 29, 1951 and July 8, 1954, p. 10. West, G. M. 1960 (4th edition). *St Andrews Florida*. St. Andrew, FL: Panama City Publishing Company, p. 15. S. P. Davis' homestead claim was #06876 issued by the registrar at the land office in Gainesville, Florida, March 30, 1917, signed for Pres. Woodrow Wilson by Secretary W. P. LeRoy, recorded patent number 574413. This paper is now in the personal collection of Pasco Hillard Cain.

9   6   "old ship's pass ... new ship's pass" Womack (1994), pp. 19-20, 144-145.

9   7   "Panama City Beach" Bell (1961), p. 195. Hutchison (1951-54) pp. 24, 139-149. West (1960), p. 4. Our attitude toward the poor farmland and lack of fresh water on the beaches was noticed by others: "The old time Florida Cracker stayed away from the beaches." Fuller, Walter P. 1954. *This was Florida's Boom*. St. Petersburg, FL: Times Publishing Co., pp. 44-45.

9   8   "we had to tack a sailboat" Bell (1961), p. 59.

9   9   "nearest neighbors" The two brothers and three sisters are Roy David

Daniels, Steve Daniels, Laurene Langley, Joyce P. Smith, and Iva Dearinger.

9   10 "the mailboat" Bell (1961) p. 63. Hutchison (1951-54) pp. 31-32. Moroney, Rita L. 1985. *History of the U.S. Postal Service, 1775-1984*. Washington, DC: U.S. Government Printing Office: 1990-257-497/20076, pp. 2-3. Womack (1994), p. 64.

10   11 "Wetappo, Allanton ... Farmdale ... Belle Isle ... Auburn (Florida) ... Callaway ... San Blas ... Cromanton ... Parker ... Millville ... Overstreet" Bell (1961), pp. 59, 76-77. Hutchison (1951-54), pp. 10 and 23. Womack (1994), pp. 53, 80-81.

10   12 "Dr. D. M. Adams, Sr." A clear picture of Doc Adams is found in Bell (1963), p. 33 (unnumbered). See also Bell (1961) p. 222. Womack (1994), p. 116.

10   13 "could we exchange me for a doll" Interview with Eloise Davis Cain, October, 1989.

11   14 "Mama gleaned the real story" Interview with Eloise Cain Davis, June, 1994.

11   15 "Uncle George ... Uncle John ... Uncle Mood" Bell (1961) pp. 50, 181. Hutchison (1951-54) p. 23.

11   16 "a military pension for Mama's father" James Russell of Farmdale, Florida, also known as James R. Hallam, filed a Soldiers' Pension Claim Under the Act of 1913 with Confederate Pension #8501 on May 7, 1920. It was approved October 20, 1920, with pay from May 7, 1920, on the basis of his service in Co. K, 2nd Regiment of Kentucky in the C.S.A. from June 1861 to his capture after a muster roll of October 31, 1864, and subsequent escape to serve with Brig. Gen. Basil W. Duke until April 30, 1865.

112   17 "One of these girls was my mother" National Society of Daughters of the American Revolution (DAR) records of Eleanor Hallam Davis, National No. 582229.

12   18 "Hallams welcomed Mama" Eleanor Hallam Davis was admitted to the Keturah Moss Chapter of the DAR on October 11, 1973, the chapter of her cousin Elizabeth Voorhees Cooley (Mrs. Frank E. Cooley, Jr.) of Fort Thomas, KY.

12   19 "Crooked Island Sound" Interview with Eleanor Russell Hallam Davis, March, 1972. Bell (1961), p. 5. *Golden Anniversary Celebration, Gulf County, Florida* (1975), p. 47. West (1960), p. 15.

Wanting More

13   20 "Cullen Raffield's boat" Bell (1961) p. 90. *Golden Anniversary Celebration, Gulf County, Florida* (1975), p. 32. In 1894, mullet runs of 100,000 lbs. in a morning were common for the fishing grounds from Cook Bayou off East St. Andrew's Bay to Sand Island off Apalachicola, Florida. Womack (1994), pp. 50, 54, 83, 90.

13   21 "Uncle Higdon Stone on the deck of the schooner" Bell (1961), pp. 95-96, 100, 103, 105-108. This schooner was probably Terrel Higdon Stone's Miss Steppie, see *Golden Anniversary Celebration, Gulf County, Florida* (1975), p. 16

13   22 "George Hardy" Golden Anniversary Celebration, Gulf County, Florida (1975), pp. 18, 30.
13   23 "George Hardy and Uncle Hig" *Golden Anniversary Celebration, Gulf County, Florida* (1975), p. 29.

13   24 "150 foot steamer Tarpon" The Tarpon was built in 1888 at Wilmington, Delaware, and put into service by a Pensacola, Florida, company for weekly runs to St. Andrew's Bay, Apalachicola, Carrabelle, and back to Pensacola, by about 1900. She went down September 1, 1937, in a gale between Pensacola and St. Andrew's Bay. Her captain, W. G. Barrow, was lost with her. Bell (1963), p. 27. Hutchison (1951-1954) pp. 46-47, 51-52. West (1960), pp. 14-15. Womack (1994), pp. 147, 149.

13   25 "turpentining" Blount, Robert S. III. 1993. Spirits of Turpentine, a history of Florida naval stores 1528-1950. Florida Heritage Journal Monograph No. 3. Tallahassee, FL: Florida Agricultural Museum. For stills, saw mills, and lumber companies, see also: Bell (1961), pp. 5, 64, 124, 179-181, 193-197. Hutchison (1951-54), pp. 102-104. Womack (1994), p. 59.

13   26 "species of pine in Florida" Pinus elliotti (slash), Pinus palustris (longleaf), Pinus taeda (loblolly), Pinus echinata (shortleaf), Pinus rigida serotina (pond), Pinus clausa (sand), Pinus glabra (spruce), Pinus elliotti var densa (South Florida slash). Only slash and longleaf pines run gum in commercial quantities.

13   27 "cup ... hack ... face cut" Blount (1993), pp. 25, 32, 35-37, 48.

14   28 "pulling the boxes" Blount (1993), pp. 37-39, 49, 52-53.

14   29 "emptied the buckets" Blount (1993), pp. 36-37, 39, 49. Womack (1994), p. 94.

15   30 "the turpentine still" Blount (1993), pp. 23, 41-44, 50, 58.

15   31 "scrape the boxes" Blount (1993), pp. 40, 49, 56.

15   32 "naval stores" Bell (1961), pp. 124, 179-181. Blount (1993), pp. 8-46. *Golden Anniversary Celebration, Gulf County, Florida* (1975), p. 28. Oliver, William F. 1948. "Recent developments in naval stores operation." *Slash Pine Cache 1948.* Gainesville, FL: Forestry Club of the University of Florida. Womack (1994), pp. 65, 82. The naval stores industry in Florida was once "the world's largest exporter of turpentine and rosin," Blount (1993), pp. 2-32. Naval stores included timber from the largest of the native oaks in West Florida. See Wood, Virginia S. 1981. *Live Oaking: southern timber for tall ships.* Boston: Northwestern University. Turpentining circa 1996 — a hole is drilled in the base of a gum running pine, and the mouth of a two liter carbonated-drink bottle is inserted into the hole. About six weeks later, the bottle full of pine gum is removed. This way there is no need to cut the face of a tree to extract its sap. Research is underway to make bottles from a resin, so the gum would not have to be removed from the bottle, and it could be melted in the cooker without contaminating the resin.

15   33 "WSM radio station" Doyle, Don H. 1985. *Nashville in the New South 1880-1930.* Knoxville, TN: University of Tennessee Press, pp. 197, 215-216.
        Early Forestry

20   34 "worked out the trees for turpentine" Bell (1961), pp. 170-181. Blount (1993), pp. 45-46.

20   35 "Daddy worked for good wages as a rafter" Blount (1993), pp. 3, 26.

20   36 "pulpwood" Bell (1961), pp. 182-183.

20   37 "five kinds of poisonous snakes" Crotalus adamanteus and Crotalus

atricaudatus (eastern diamondback and cane-brake rattlesnakes), Agkistrodon piscivorus (water moccasin), Agkistrodon contortrix (copperhead), Micrurus fulvius (coral snake).

20   38 "cutting in a profligate way" Bell (1961), pp. 179-181. Blount (1993), pp. 3, 45-46. Womack (1994), pp. 41, 82, 138-139. *Fire Fighter's Guide, training manual*. 1983. Tallahassee, FL: Florida Department of Agriculture and Consumer Services, p. 1.

21   39 "Florida in 1925" Fuller (1954), pp. 54-64.

21   40 "no jobs at all" Fuller, Walter P. 1972. *St. Petersburg and Its People*. St. Petersburg, FL: Great Outdoors Publishing Co. pp. 186-189.

21   41 "faculty trained ... at Biltmore" Gifford Pinchot was succeeded by Dr. Carl A. Schenck as manager of the forest estate of Mr. George Vanderbilt. Schenck developed the work of the Biltmore School of Forestry that he organized in 1898. The School was discontinued in 1912. Newins, H. S. "The Life of Austin Carey" [sic]. 1949. *Slash Pine Cache 1949*. Gainesville, FL: Forestry Club of the University of Florida, pp. 21-22, 55-57.

The Great Depression

22   42 "lack of money altogether" the shrinkage of money through bank failures in one part of Florida is recorded in Fuller (1954), pp. 54-55.

22   43 "Under President Herbert Hoover" Guerrant, Edward O. 1960. *Herbert Hoover: Franklin Roosevelt, comparisons and contrasts*. Cleveland, OH: H. Allen. Smith, Gene. 1970. *Herbert Hoover and the Great Depression*. New York: Morrow. Terkel, Studs. 1970. *Hard Times, an oral history of the great depression*. New York: Pantheon Books.

22   44 "scrip good only at some grocery stores" Fuller (1954), pp. 186, 189.

23   45 "In 1926 ... In 1928" Bell (1961), p. 143. Bell (1963), pp. 15-17.

23   46 "Roosevelt became President" Davis, Kenneth S. 1985. *FDR, the New York years 1928-1933*. New York: Random House. Davis, Kenneth S. 1986. *FDR, the New Deal years 1933-1937*. New York: Random House. Perkins,

Frances. 1946. *The Roosevelt I Knew*. New York: The Viking Press.

23   47 "With government priming the pump" We were directly affected by
national forestry policy from 1932 to 1941, as summarized in Owen, A. L. Riesch.
1983. *Conservation Under FDR*. New York: Praeger Publishers, pp. 16-18.

23   48 "paved Highway 98" Womack (1994), pp. 117, 125.

23   49 "Bay High School" Bell (1961), p. 124. Hutchison (1951-54), p. 113.

23   50 "favorable laws for tree-farming" Passage of the Cooperative Farm
Forestry Act, May 18, 1937, increased technical aid for timber woodlands
management to farm owners. Owen (1983), p. 123.

23   51 "Florida Forest Service" Federal timberland purchases authorized by
Congress went from 14,727,680 acres in 1933 to 117,497,531 acres in 1941. The
Fulmer Act of 1935 sponsored the expansion of state forests. Conservation of
privately held timberlands was encouraged by Congressional programs of
research, fire protection, and establishing Divisions of State and Private Forestry
in the federal Forest Service. Owen (1983), p. 107.

War Clouds and the Civilian

24   52 "the greatest 'adventure' of the twentieth century was headed my way"
Morison, Samuel Eliot. 1947-1962. *History of United States Naval Operations in
World War II*, 15 Vols. Boston: Little Brown and Co., is the definitive source for
the naval war in the Pacific. A one volume alternative for the interested reader is
Spector, Ronald H. 1985. *The American War with Japan, Eagle Against the Sun*.
New York: The Free Press.

24   53 "Pensacola" Turnbull, Capt. Archibald D., and Lord, Lt. Cdr. Clifford L.
1949. *History of United States Naval Aviation*. New Haven: Yale University Press,
pp. 38, 66-67, 100.

25   54 "we knew war was coming" Davis, Kenneth S. 1993. *FDR, into the
storm 1937-1940*. New York: Random House.

Early Conservation

26   55 "Civilian Conservation Corps" Davis (1979), pp. 77-79. Larrabee, Eric.

1987. Commander in Chief, Franklin Delano Roosevelt, his lieutenants, and their war. New York: Harper & Row Publishers, pp. 107-108. Owen (1983), pp. 83-84, 106, 128-144.

26   56 "share-cropping system in the South" See: Conrad, David Eugene. 1965. The Forgotten Farmers, the story of sharecroppers in the New Deal. Urbana, IL: University of Illinois Press. The Disinherited Speak, letters from sharecroppers. 1937. New York: The Workers Defense League for the Southern Tenant Farmers' Union.

27   57 "they had not lived this well in years" Interview with Dalton Clyde Spann, Summer, 1993.

The US Blackwater

27   58 "the US *Blackwater*" Bell (1961), pp. 50, 58, 226.

27   59 "dredging" Womack (1994), pp. 76-77.

2   60 "seaplanes docked" See photographs of flying boats in these years in Turnbull and Lord (1949), between pages 192 and 193. Seaplanes from 1903 to 1953 are described and illustrated in Knott, Capt. Richard C. 1979. *The American Flying Boat*. Annapolis, MD: Naval Institute Press.

29   61 "seaplanes ... taking off and landing" On November 29, 1910, Glenn Curtiss offered to train a U.S. Navy officer in a Curtiss plane at no cost. The navy accepted the offer to train Lt. Theodore G. Ellyson who became Naval Aviator No. 1. His roommate at the Naval Academy was Chester W. Nimitz. The first seaplanes were allocated in the U.S. Navy was early as 1916. The first flying boat unit was of the U.S. Marines in Culebra, Puerto Rico. Turnbull and Lord (1949), pp. 12, 39, 72-74.

30   62 "canal past Overstreet, Florida" *Golden Anniversary Celebration, Gulf County, Florida* (1975), p. 29. Womack (1994), p. 77.

31   63 "Wewahitchka" Bell (1961), p. 128.

31   64 "Alton's unit was less than two years old" The Florida Society of American Foresters published histories of early 20th century forestry practices. See a list of these in Grosenbaugh, Lewis R. 1983. *History of the Florida Society*

of American Foresters. Gainesville, FL: The Florida Society of American Foresters, SAF 83-10.

Ranger Sam

32   65 "survey a site for the forestry tower" Owen (1983), p. 107.

33   66 "Red Fish Point" Womack (1994), pp. 91, 101-103.

33   67 "cattlemen ran their cattle" Akerman, Joe A., Jr. 1976. *Florida Cowman, a history of Florida cattle raising*. Kissimmee, FL: Florida Cattlemen's Association. Cattle came to Florida with Ponce de Leon in 1521. We were in a long line of cattlemen and women — Spanish, indigenous Americans, British, later European immigrants, Seminoles, African-Americans, Cuban-Americans — to the present. pp. 204-207, 266, 281 — Our cattle were descendants of smaller, leaner, Spanish cattle who had adapted for centuries to our climate and terrain. pp. 59-60, 86, 200-201 — We were Crackers. I was always told that we were given that name by townspeople and visitors who saw us herding our cattle with whips that made a sharp CRACK sound when used. Posed photographs from the Civil War period show men of few possessions holding their whips like kings with scepters. The name Cracker was used by visitors to Florida for the European-Americans there from the 1700s onward. p. 108 — As with Jacob Summerlin of Punta Rassa, Florida, to us "the word cracker implied honesty, hard work, genuineness and a certain provincial shrewdness."

33   68 "cattlemen's range fires" *Slash Pine Cache 1949*. Dean Newins of the Forestry School quoted the highly respected Austin Cary, "there is a field in the forests of the South for the use of fire for both protection and silvicultural purposes." p. 57.

34   69 "Farmdale tower" *Golden Anniversary Celebration, Gulf County, Florida* (1975), p. 31.

34   70 "George Toepher" Bell (1961), p. 168.

Forest Protection

35   71 "Forest Service work in fire control and forest conservation" *Fire Fighter's Guide, training manual* (1983), was written under the direction of John

M. Bethea to compile the methods developed in the 20th century by a generation of Florida Forest Service foresters then retiring. A "History of fire control, state of Florida" is given on two unnumbered pages before the table of contents. A glossary of terms is given on p. 155.

46   72 "fire line" *Fire Fighter's Guide, training manual* (1983), pp. 117-122.

Leaving Home

38   73 "the draft" The work of Gen. George C. Marshall in raising a citizen's military led by competent professionals cannot be underestimated. Larrabee (1987), pp. 108-121. See also: Parrish, Thomas D. 1989. *Roosevelt and Marshall, partners in politics and war.* New York: William Morrow and Company. Stoler, Mark A. 1989. *George C. Marshall, a soldier-statesman of the American century.* Boston: Twayne Publishers.

38   74 "Harold S. Newins" *Seminole 1941.* Yearbook of the University of Florida.

Leaving the Port St. Joe Forestry Unit

39   75 "tractor and fire line plow" *Fire Fighter's Guide, training manual* (1983), pp. 32-33, 35.

39   76 "Settlemire four-disc plow" Warren Settlemire perfected the first tractor drawn fire line plow at the Florida Forest Service shops in Lake City, Florida, in the early 1930s. He made a four disc plow from disc parts, two turned in one direction and two in the other, with a middle-buster (a turning plow) between them. The soil is cut with the discs and turned over behind the middle buster, so plants that would feed a fire are buried. See an illustration in *Fire Fighter's Guide, training manual* (1983), p. 35.

40   77 "Gary's transport truck" Such trucks transported our tractors. See illustrations in *Fire Fighter's Guide, training manual* (1983), p. 32.

The CLO House

41   78 "1940, Japan" Hoyt, Edwin P. 1986. *Japan's War, the great Pacific conflict* 1853-1952. New York: McGraw-Hill Book Company pp. 1-233. Spector (1978), pp. 33-53. See also: Thorne, Christopher. 1978. *Allies of a Kind, the*

United States, Britain and the war against Japan. New York: Oxford University Press.

41   79 "lend-lease" Pres. Franklin D. Roosevelt explained complicated policies in terms ordinary citizens understood. See local reaction to the Lend-Lease explanation in Brinkley, D. 1988. *Washington Goes to War.* Ballantine Books, New York, pp. 47-49. Pres. Roosevelt's speeches reached most Americans on the radio, see Roosevelt, Franklin D. Russell D. Buhite and David W. Levy (Ed.s) 1992. *FDR's Fireside Chats.* Norman OK: University of Oklahoma Press. Congress approved the Lend-Lease in March, 1941. Larrabee (1987), pp. 36-37, 41-43, 50. See also Kimball, Warren F. 1969. *The Most Unsordid Act, lend-lease, 1939-1941.* Baltimore, MD: Johns Hopkins Press.

42-43   80   "Joe Busby and Bill McCown ... and Paul Sims ... Pat Hunter, Woodrow "Coon Bottom" Glen, and Johnny Mac Brown" All are pictured on the page devoted to the CLO House in the *Seminole 1941.*

Leaving Farmdale

44   81 "taking Daddy's homestead" Bell (1961), pp. 186-192. On April 24, 1941, the U.S. War Department ordered construction of a gunnery school. On May 1, 1941, Col. W. A. Maxwell arrived on the peninsula of East St. Andrew's Bay as project officer. May 6, 1941, a Declaration of Taking was filed in federal court in Pensacola. On May 22, 1941, East Bay residents were told "they had until July 7 to vacate their land. Departing residents were instructed to take only personal belongings and furnishings. When they left, they were advised to turn in their house keys at the main gate." Womack (1994), pp. 155-156.

44   82 "round up cattle" Eloise Davis Cain in 1994 remembers Col. Maxwell, "I went to see him for an extension beyond the six weeks they gave us. My folks had lived on Daddy's homestead 30 years. They were supposed to gather all their things and leave, with no money. He told me there would be no extension. If my folks didn't leave by the deadline, his soldiers would pitch all their furniture out in the yard and shoot down all their cattle out in the woods." The Davises would never go back to the life they had known at Farmdale. Akerman (1976), pp. 126-137.

44   83 "The ferry" Womack (1994), p. 40.

45   84 "Duck" Samuel A. Davis was a Cracker on a Cracker Pony. See Akerman (1976), pp. 187-193.

Tyndall Field

46   85 "Tyndall" Bell (1961), pp. 1868-192. On May 15, 1941, Congressman Bob Sikes suggested to the U.S. War Department that the new gunnery school be named Tyndall Field in honor of World War I ace Lt. Frank B. Tyndall. Womack (1994), pp. 155, 158-160, 162.

The Draft

52   86 "Civilian Pilot Training (CPT)" Pisano, Dominick A. 1994. *To Fill the Skies with Pilots*, the civilian pilot training program 1939-46. Urbana & Chicago: University of Illinois Press, pp. 1-84. Samuel A. Davis was issued Commercial-CPT student pilot certificate No. S 351917, dated September 22, 1941, from the Civil Aeronautics Authority.

52   87 "J. E. Churchwell" Womack (1994), p. 111.

The War in Gainesville, Florida

54   88 "All of Europe and half of Asia" Keegan, John. 1989. *The Second World War.* New York: Viking, pp. 10-290. Newton, Wesley Phillips, and Rea, Robert S. (Ed.) 1987. *Wings of Gold, an account of naval aviation training in World War II.* Tuscaloosa, AL: The University of Alabama Press, pp. 52-61.

55   89 "December 7, 1941" Buell, Harold L. 1990. *Dauntless Helldivers, a dive-bomber pilot's epic story of the carrier battles.* New York: Orion Books, pp. 42-43. Hoyt (1986), pp. 223-285. Keegan (1989), pp. 240-251. Karig, Cdr. Walter, USNR, and Kelley, Lt. Welbourn, USNR. 1944. *Battle Report, Pearl Harbor to Coral Sea.* New York: Rinehart & Company, Inc., pp. 5-119.   Potter, E. B. 1976. Nimitz. Annapolis: U.S. Naval Institute.   Prange, Gordon W. 1981. *At Dawn We Slept, the untold story of Pearl Harbor.* New York: Penguin Books. Spector (1985), pp. 1-8, 79-84, 93-100. Terkel, Studs. 1984. *The Good War, an oral history of World War Two.* New York: Pantheon Press, pp. 19-37. Weintraub, Stanley. 1991. *Long Day's Journey into War, December 7, 1941.* New York: Truman Talley Books, Dutton.

55   90 "SNJ" Leuthner, Stuart, and Jensen, Oliver. 1992. *High Honor.*

Washington, DC: Smithsonian Institution Press, p. 398. Swanborough, Gordon, and Bowers, Peter M. 1968. *United States Aircraft Since 1911*. New York: Funk & Wagnalls, pp. 321-322.

55   91 "Naval Air Station at Jacksonville" Buell (1990), pp. 21-22.

56   92 "two years college requirement" pp. 57-59 of Bradford, Cdr. John W. Jr., USN (Ret.) 1994. "In pursuit of gold wings." *Foundation*, vol. 15, no. 2, pp. 56-64. Quinn, David C. 1989. "Never a dull moment." in Leuthner, Stuart, and Jensen, Oliver (Eds.) *High Honor*. Washington DC: Smithsonian Institution Press, p. 94.

New Places

57   93 "the death of a son" Weatherford, Dorothy. 1990. *American Women and World War II*. New York: Facts on File, pp. 285-303.

58   94 "N3N" This was "the last bi-plane to serve in the U.S. Navy." Swanborough and Bowers, pp. 306, 318-320.

58   95 (Boeing) "Stearman Trainer" Swanborough and Bowers (1968), pp. 357-358.

59   96 "an aerobatic routine" For the usefulness of aerobatic flying in war, see Churchill, Jan. 1992. *On Wings of War, Teresa James aviator*. Manhattan, KS: Sunflower University Press. For a description of these aerobatic routines, see: Hynes, Samuel. 1988. Flights of Passage. New York: Frederic C. Beil, pp. 51-52. and Newton and Rea (1987), pp. 311-313.

New Faces

61   97 "differences among people" For an idea of the variety of people encountered in World War II, note the biographies of the speakers in Terkel (1984). The experience of men and women new to the armed services was similar. See Weatherford (1990), pp. 48-79.

61   98 "Texans" For a description of Texas up to the time Samuel A. Davis went to Lew Foote's Field in Dallas, see *Texas, A Guide to the Lone Star State*. 1940. compiled by Workers in the Writers' Program of the Work Project Administration in the State of Texas. New York: Hastings House, "Corpus Christi" pp.

215-223, "Dallas" pp. 224-241, "Tour 25, Rosenburg-Victoria-Alice-Laredo" pp. 645-651, "Tour 26, San Antonio-Kenedy-Beeville-Corpus Christi" pp. 652-655.

61   99 "Corpus Christi" The Naval Air Station is described in *The Mark III Slipstream* from the 1940s, published by Aviation Cadet Regiment, U.S. Naval Air Training Center. It is inscribed "Navy wings for victory — ashore, afloat, aloft" and "Dedicated to the Navy men on the ground." Samuel A. Davis is pictured as a cadet is on page 251 of the issue for his class.

Texas Women

64   100 "plenty of red stamps for gas" Weatherford (1990), pp. 200-216.

The Fifth Woman

66   101 "Lou Gehrig's disease" The Iron Man of the New York Yankees baseball club died of amyotrophic lateral sclerosis in the 1930s, hence the common name "Lou Gehrig's disease."

60   102 "Odem ... Edroy ... Sinton" The Forgy Farm in 1996 still has a Sinton telephone, an Odem address, and an Edroy interstate highway exit. See *San Patricio County in 1976*, a bicentennial perspective. 1976. Sinton, TX: Sinton Bicentennial Celebrations, Inc., pp. 13-15, 33, 45-46.

67   103 "This landlady" See Ivins, Molly. 1991. "Texas Women: True Grit and All the Rest" in *Molly Ivins Can't Say That, Can She?*. New York: Random House, pp. 165-170.

Those Golden Wings

68   104 "operational phase training" An extensive account of similar naval aviation training is found in the edited letters of then Cadet/Ensign Robert S. Rea, in Newton and Rea (1987).

68   105 "PBY" *Jane's Fighting Aircraft of World War II*. 1946-47, 1989, 1992, 1994. New York: Crescent Books. p. 218. Swanborough and Bowers (1968), pp. 76-80.

68   106 "PBM" *Jane's* (1994), p. 245. Swanborough and Bowers (1968), pp. 298-300. Pratt & Whitney R-2800-22 or -34 engines: *Jane's* (1994), p. 311.

Swanborough and Bowers (1968), p. 300. Seaplane pilot's preference for PBM: Quinn (1989), p. 96.

Cadets and Instructors

74   107 "Torpedo Squadron 8" Gay, George. 1979. *Sole Survivor, the battle of Midway and its effect on his life.* Jersey City, NJ: 3B Litho.

My Last Love

78   108 "Moral Dee" Interview with Marianne Theile Forgy and Paul Berthold Forgy, July, 1994.

78   109 "He bought 305 acres" Lea, Tom. 1957. *The King Ranch*. Boston: Little, Brown. Powers, Elmer G. "Day by day on the farm, 1937." In Kyvig, David E. (Ed.) 1976. *FDR's America*. St. Charles, MO: Forum Press, pp. 80-95. At the time Mr. Forgy bought the land, it was believed by some that the black land was not good for framing. Mr. Forgy was a carpenter, but he told his daughter that you could not get ahead unless you invested your money. To this day, his investment in this land gives top yields in cotton and sorghum grain. See *San Patricio County in 1976, a bicentennial perspective* (1976), p. 13.

78   110 "was called 'Lona'" Mary Lona Forgy Davis is the daughter of Lona Frances Bozarth. The family story is that an Uncle in the early 19th century loved a young woman named Lona, who died during their engagement and was buried in her wedding dress. He later married a most understanding woman, because she agreed to name their first daughter "Lona" at his request. The name came down until their grandaughter, Lona Corn, had no daughters, so it went to her niece Lona Frances Bozarth. Our first daughter was named Lona Frances Davis, but she has no daughters and no nieces from our family. She is the fifth and perhaps the last Lona in this line, unless her son Jonathan has a daughter named Lona in his future.

79   111 "saw them through the 1930s" Davis (1979), pp. 68-76, 617-618. Fusfeld, Daniel R. 1956. *The Economic Thought of Franklin D. Roosevelt and the Origins of the New Deal.* New York: Columbia University Press, pp. 234-237.

79   112 "the oldest, Paul" Interview with Marianne Thiele and Paul Berthold Forgy, July, 1994.

80   113 "Rawlings' book" Rawlings, Marjorie Kinnan. 1938. *The Yearling*.
New York: Charles Scribner's Sons. See also: Parker, Idella, with Keating, Mary.
1992. *Idella, Marjorie Kinnan Rawlings' "perfect maid"*. Gainesville, FL:
University Press of Florida. Silverthorne, Elizabeth. 1988. *Marjorie Kinnan
Rawlings, sojourner at Cross Creek*. Woodstock, NY: Overlook Press.

80   114 "traced the Forgys" Wallace, Lucille Forgy. *Forgy, Forgey, and Forgie
Family History*. Privately published, in the collection of Lona Davis Spencer.

80   115 "our common heritage" In fact, the first recorded visit of a European to
what became Bay County, Florida, and San Patricio Countyu, Texas, was made by
the same man. Alvar Nunez Cabeza de Vaca of Spain passed through what
became Bay County, Florida, in 1528 and through what became San Patricio
County, Texas, in 1535. *The Journey of Alvar Nunez Cabeza de Vaca and his
companions from Florida to the Pacific, 1528-1536*. Translated from his own
narrative by Fanny Bandelier, together with the report of Father Marcos of Nizza
and a letter from the viceroy Mendoza. New York: A.S. Barnes & Company
(1905); Allerton Book Co. (1922); AMS Press (1973).

80   116 "Henry Flagler" Chandler, David Leon. 1986. *Henry Flagler, the
astonishing life and times of the visionary robber baron who founded Florida*.
New York: Macmillan. Martin, Sidney Walter. 1949. *Florida's Flagler*. Athens,
GA: University of Georgia Press.

War Time Marriage

81   117 "we planned to get married" See Weatherford (1990), pp. 243-264.

82   118 "the financial relationships in the area switched" *San Patricio County
in 1976, a bicentennial perspective* (1976), p. 15. For a summary discussion of
oil's effect on the socioeconomic life in Texas, see: Gillete, Michael L. 1986.
Texas in Transition. Austin, TX: Lyndon Baines Johnson Library, School of Public
Affairs, and Foundation.

83   119 "Sid Rigell" Rigell, Joseph S. and Rigell, Elizabeth W. 1992. *Fired
Again and Again, Praise the Lord!* Baltimore, MD: The Afikomen Company, pp.
34-36.

84   120 "all the saints preserve us" Interview with Donald Hugh Flaherty, October, 1989.

85   121"ready room" Every squadron of pilots had one at every air field. See Hynes (1988), pp. 131-132.

85   122 "this guy has a lot of confidence in me" Interview with Carl Mervin "Tuck" Dicken, October, 1993.

85   123 "Martin" Gunston, Bill. 1994. *World Encyclopedia of Aircraft Manufacturers*. Annapolis, MD: Naval Institute Press, pp. 196-197.

Brotherly Love

86   124 "flight to Coco Solo" Personnel of VP/VPB-33 with Mueller, Lt. A. J. USNR (Ret.) 1992. *Black Cats with Wings of Gold*. Philadelphia: Smith-Edwards-Dunlap Co., pp. 4-8.

86   125 "seaplanes in the Caribbean" Personnel of VP/VPB-33 with Mueller (1992), pp. 1-10.

87   126 "limits of our red stamps" Weatherford (1990), pp. 200-216.

87   127 "beaches... famous for their slaughter" Pyle, Ernie. 1944. *Brave Men*. New York: Henry Holt and Company, Inc. pp. 13-199.

88   128 "landings under heavy fire" Sidey, Hugh. "D-Day, the home front." Time, June 13, 1994, pp. 48-49. Strahan, Jerry E. 1994. *Andrew Jackson Higgins and the Boats That Won World War II*. Baton Rouge, LA: Louisiana State University Press. Keegan (1989), p. 562.

89   129 "another casualty of war" Asbell, Bernard. 1969. *When FDR Died*. New York: Holt, Rinehart and Winston. Bishop, Jim. 1974. *FDR's Last Year, April 1944-April 1945*. New York: William Morrow. Freidel, Frank. 1973. *Franklin D. Roosevelt*. Vols. 1-4. Boston: Little, Brown and Company. On April 13, 1945, Pres. Harry S. Truman met with the highest military leaders of the U.S. for the first time. They told him that Germany would not be defeated for another

six months. They expected Japan would not be defeated for another year and a half. Truman, Harry S. 1955. *Memoirs by Harry S. Truman, Year of Decisions.* New York: Doubleday & Company, Inc., p. 17.

Good-Bye

94   130 "flight to Kaneohe" Davis, Samuel A. *Aviators Flight Log Book #1.* October 10, 1942 through May 31, 1946.

94   131 "the vast Pacific" Pyle, Ernie. 1946. *Last Chapter.* New York: Henry Holt and Company. This posthumously published work contains Pyle's experiences in the Pacific War before his death from a sniper's bullet April 18, 1945, on Ie Shima.

95   132 "dried the tears they would not let us see" Interview with Evelyn Dicken, July, 1993. See also: Weatherford (1990), pp. 265-284.

Loss and Replacement

95   133 "On July 10, 1945" Davis, Flight Log #1

95   134 "Okinawa was secured" Hoyt (1985), p. 391. Mason (1986), pp. 333-335. Spector (1985), pp. 532-540.

96   135 "Buckner Bay" Karig, Harris, and Manson (1949), pp. 415-417 and 427-428. Spector (1985), pp. 534-535, 539-540.

96   136 "USS *Pine Island*" Litz, Leo M. 1946. *Report from the Pacific.* Indianapolis: *The Indianapolis News*, pp. 288-297. Quinn (1992), p. 101.

97   137 "cheery letter ... But his wife Louise told us" Interview with Louise E. Reid, October, 1993.

97   138 "two ex-PBY pilots now flying this PBM" Interview with Raymond J. Lutz, October, 1993.

At the Front

98   139 "July 18, 1945" Davis, Flight Log #1.

100   140 "pick up some debris" Davis, Flight Log #1.

100   141 "people who knew what we were up against" Litz, pp. 290-191.

On Call

101   142 "Halsey's Third Fleet Carrier Task Force" Davis, Flight Log #1. See also Halsey, William F. and Bryan, Joseph. 1947. *Admiral Halsey's Story*. New York: Whittlesey House.

Inside Japan

102   143 "within sight of pedestrians" Litz (1946), pp. 288-289. Quinn (1989), pp. 97-98.

102   144 (Grumman) "F6F" *Jane's* (1994), pp. 233-234. Swanborough and Bowers (1968), pp. 216-218.

102   145 "USS *Bonhomme Richard*" Karig, Harris, and Manson (1949), pp. 478-488. Sowinski, Larry. 1981. *Action in the Pacific, as seen by U.S. Navy photographers during World War 2*. Annapolis, MD: Naval Institute Press, pp. 185-191.

1104 146 "massive losses ... to kamikaze attackers" Karig, Harris, and Manson (1949), pp. 379-391. Specific losses of material and lives are given in Keegan (1989), pp. 566-573.

Finding Yoder

105   147 "planed up on the step" There is a picture of a "Martin flying boat" at the point of planing up on its step on page 405 of Colton, F. Barrows. 1940. "Aviation in commerce and defense." *The National Geographic Magazine*. vol. 78, no. 6, December, 1940, pp. 685-726.

106   148 "Allied underground in China" Litz (1946), pp. 298-299.

106   149 "detected as an alien" Quinn (1992), p. 97.

107   150 "our submarines" Karig, Harris, and Manson (1949), p. 392. Ramage, Vice Adm. Lawson P. "Wolf packs on the prowl" in Mason (1986), pp. 221-232.

107   151 "Ensign George Herbert Walker Bush" McCombs, Don and Worth, Fred L. 1983. *World War II, 4,139 strange and fascinating facts*. New York: Wings Books, p. 87.

109   152 "Mitsubishi" Gunston (1993), p. 207.

109   153 "General Douglas MacArthur and Admiral Chester W. Nimitz" *Nimitz* by Potter, (1976). Manchester, William. 1978. *American Caesar*. New York: Dell Publishing Co. Manchester dedicated this book "To the 29th Marines, 3,612 landed on Okinawa April 1, 1945, 2,821 fell in 82 days, the highest price ever paid by a U.S. Marine Corps regiment in a single battle."

109   154 "PB2Y" *Jane's* (1994), p. 218. Swanborough and Bowers (1968), pp. 81-82. Personnel of VP/VPB-33 with Mueller (1992), pp. 11-118. Knott, Richard. 1984. *Black Cat Raiders of WW II*. Zebra.

Finding Smith and Selway

111   155 "we began to hear a message repeated" Karig, Capt. Walter, Harris, Lt. Cdr. Russell L., Manson, Lt. Cdr. Frank A. 1949. *Battle Report, Victory in the Pacific*. New York: Rinehart and Company, pp. 486-487. The authors do not identify Crew 5 of the Willie-7, they do not report that Smith and Selway were forced to leave us up inside Japan alone, and it was not the case the "All three planes put down easily." However, the mission is in the context of the Third Fleet accurately.

The Valley of the Shadow of Death

117   156 "praying together" Interview with Donald Hugh Flaherty and Raymond J. Lutz, October, 1993.

Too Late

127   157 "taxied a crippled PBM for 26 hours" Quinn (1989) remembers a VH-3 PBM that was taxied 150 miles to save the lives of the crew and survivors, though

"They had to junk the plane, but [Jim Blumenstock] got back. That was the capability of that airplane. Just marvelous." p. 99.

127 158 "blow us out of the sky" The Willie 7 closely resembled an approaching kamikaze. See: Karig, Harris, and Manson, pp. 379-391. Keegan, pp. 567-573. Spector, pp. 536-539.

Muddy Waters

131 159 "stayed ... all those hours" Litz (1946), p. 296.

Daddy's Thin Line

132 160 "Capt. Erdmann" Litz (1946), pp. 286-297. See also: Litz, Leo. "Report from the Pacific" column in *The Indianapolis News*, August 7, 1945, pp. 1 and 3.

134 161 "the ward room filled up" Litz (1946), p. 294.

135 162 "when we fought the whole population" The Allies experienced significant Japanese resistance to our advance on Iwo Jima and Okinawa. See: Karig, Harris, and Manson, pp. 279-318, 349-440. Spector, pp. 494-503, 532-540. Potter (1976), concludes that Samurai tradition "made it impossible for the Japanese to acknowledge defeat. The peace feelers they had put out through the Soviet government were designed to achieve two things at the same time — to get terms short of unconditional surrender from the Allies and to keep Russia out of the Pacific war." pp. 385-386.

Enough Gas

136 163 "back on duty" Davis, Flight Log #1.

136 164 "August 1, 1945" Davis, Flight Log #1.

The Beginning of the End

138 165 "Stalin hadn't acted surprised" McCullough, David. *Truman.* 1992. New York: Simon & Schuster, pp. 442-443. Spector (1985), pp. 553-554.

138 166 "delivered the U-235" McCullough (1992), p. 460.

138 167 "weren't out of danger" Japanese and U.S. casualties at Iwo Jima and Okinawa, especially Japanese suicides: Karig, Harris, and Manson, pp. 308, 318, 428, 430. Keegan, pp. 572-573. On June 18, 1945, the Joint Chiefs of Staff recommended to Pres. Truman that the 35% casualties in the Okinawa campaign were reasonable to expect when we invaded Kyushu in November, 1945. Their plans were to commit 767,000 troops, with 268,000 dead or wounded. Nimitz and MacArthur went on record that the invasion of Japan would be worse for the Allies than anything that had gone before, in any other theater of World War II. Spector (1985), pp. 542-545.

138 168 "Hiroshima" Professionally written first-person accounts of the Pacific island campaigns that illustrate the source of Navy and Marine response to news of the bombing of Hiroshima and Nagasaki: Fussell, Paul. "Thank God for the atomic bomb", *Washington Post*, August 23, 1981. Manchester, William. 1979. *Goodbye Darkness, a memoir of the Pacific war.* Boston: Little, Brown and Company. Though Hoyt (1986) cites the Japanese determination not to surrender (pp. 391-392), he argues that the atomic bomb was not necessary to end the Pacific war (p. 420). He argues on the basis of what the West sees as Japanese cultural fatalism. Curiously, he concludes "As it turned out, Japan could have no better friends than Douglas MacArthur and the Americans" (p. 421). Spector (1985) concludes "Whether Japan would have been eventually forced to surrender by sheer exhaustion can never be proved or disproved conclusively. Yet it is hard to see how a long-continued aerial bombardment of Japan would have cost fewer lives than the two atomic bombs." (p. 558)

Old #59081

138 169 "August 9, 1945" Davis, Flight Log #1.

139 170 "Nagasaki" Regarding a possible surrender, Hisatume Sakomizu, the Chief Secretary of the Japanese Cabinet interpreted the atom bombings: "It was not necessary to blame the military — just the atomic bomb. It was a good excuse. Someone said that the atomic bomb was the kamikaze to save Japan." Karig, Harris, and Manson (1949), pp. 429-430. The history of Japan's Supreme Council for the Direction of the War indicates that only the second atom bomb, not the first, destroyed the power of half the war ministers to argue successfully for one great last battle for Japanese honor. General Korechika Anami is quoted as saying after Hiroshima and before Nagasaki, "Would it not be wondrous for this whole nation to be destroyed like a beautiful flower?" Washington *Times*, August 6, 1985, as quoted in McCullough (1992), pp. 435-444, 453-460.

140   171 "still winning the war"   Manchester (1978), pp. 508-509.

War's End

141   172 "13th of August"   Davis, Flight Log #1.

142   173 "USS *Pennsylvania*"   In Forestry School after the War, Samuel A. Davis was telling this story out in the woods on a break. Wesley Lewis spoke up, "Not do much damage? Hell, she was sunk to the bottom till the deck was awash!" Her early career and fate are succinctly summarized in McCombs and Worth (1983), p. 461.

The C.O. Accepts a Surrender

148   174 "Japan surrendered"   Butow, Robert Joseph Charles. 1954. *Japan's Decision to Surrender.* Stanford, CA: Stanford University Press. Karig, Harris, and Manson, pp. 513-525. Manchester (1978), pp. 510-524. Spector (1985), pp. 555-560. For a primary historical account of Japanese troops' resistance to surrender, see Onoda, Hiroo. 1974. *No Surrender, my thirty-year war. Charles S. Terry* (Trans.) Tokyo: Kodansha International Ltd. (Harper & Row, distributors). Onoda remained on Lubang Island in the Philippines as a Japanese soldier until he was given oral orders to surrender by Maj. Yoshimi Taniguchi of the Japanese Chief of Staff's Headquarters on March 9, 1974.

148   175 "Truk"   Spector (1985), pp. 271-273. The island seemed important and almost impregnable before the U.S. entered World War II. Barrows (1940).

149   176 "dead reckoning ... Loran"   The textbook was Weems, Lt. Cdr. P. V. H., USN (Ret.) 1938. *Air Navigation.* 2nd. edition. New York: McGraw-Hill Book Co. Inc.

Tales of the North Pacific

150   177 "Saipan"   Hill, Adm. Harry W. "A perfect amphibious assault" in Mason (1986), pp. 246-260. Kauffman, Rear Adm. Draper. "The UDTs come of age." in Mason (1986), pp. 233-245. Manchester (1979).

152   178 "B-29 fleet took off to bomb Japan"   Edoin, Hoito. 1987. *The Night*

Tokyo Burned. New York: St. Martin's Press. Spector (1985), pp. 312-316. *Jane's* (1994), p. 209. Leuthner and Jensen (1992), p. 399. Ramer, Robert. 1992. "The whole world was on fire." in Leuthner and Jensen (1992), pp. 184-194.

152   179 "Marpi Point" Edoin, p. 183. Spector, p. 317.

Pets

153   180 "croker sack" A loosely woven heavy cloth sack used for harvesting cotton and grain crops. All the sacks we used were heavy enough to hold the goat's weight and loose enough to allow it to breathe.

Getting to Go Home

154   181 "October 11, 1945" Davis, Flight Log #1.

156   182 "not all the Army Air Corps crew was accounted for" Davis, Flight Log #1.

California Here We Come

158   183 "March 8, 1946" Davis, Flight Log #1.

Cross Country

168   184 "Aunt Sue's ranch" The Woodward Ranch was later flooded for a reservoir for Corpus Christi, Texas. The animals in the area can still be seen in the Lake Corpus Christi Sate Park, see: *TEXAS State Travel Guide.* (ca. 1993). Texas Department of Transportation, Travel and Information Division, P.O. Box 5064, Austin, Texas, 78763-5064, p. 14.

169   185 "Panama City *News Herald*" "More details on Navy exploits of Lieut. Davis." *The News Herald*, Panama City, Florida. Oct. 28, 1946, p. 8, citing the *Bermuda Mid-Ocean News.*

Admiral Forgy Davis

171   186 "May 17th" Davis, Flight Log #1.

171   187 "May 18th" Davis, Flight Log #1.

171   188 "May 19th" Davis, Flight Log #1.

171   189 "BOAC Boeing Clipper" Jane's (1994), p. 211.

172   190 "pre-World War II Boeing Clippers" See Schrader, Richard K. May, 1989. "Bridging the Atlantic." *American History Illustrated*, vol. 23, no.4, pp. 34-47.

172   191 "Mary Lona's Clipper ... flight" For a longer account of flight in the Boeing Clipper, see Follett, Ken. 1991. *Night Over Water*. New York: William Morrow and Company. Behind the dedication of the book, Follett wrote, "The flight, the passengers and the crew are all fictional. The plane is real."

Volunteered

175   192 "July 5, 1946" Davis, Samuel A. Aviators Flight Log Book #2, June 1, 1945 through December 17, 1954.

Never a Dull Day

178   193 "the body of a Navy man" Davis, Flight Log #2.

Lost and Found

181   194 "December 6, 1946" Davis, Flight Log #2.

Leaving Bermuda

186   195 "January 27, 1947" Davis, Flight Log #2.

186   196 "I flew to Norfolk to be detached" Davis, Flight Log #2.

The University of Florida

189   197 "mesquite trees being poor woods" In the 1980s, consumers would actually pay for bags of mesquite wood chips for their cooking grills, when foresters had considered these "trees" nuisances at best.

190   198 "everything else was changed" A quick comparison can be made between the University of Florida yearbook the *Seminole* of 1942 and 1949. The pictures are smaller, the pages are numbered, and women are students at Florida in 1949. For a summary of the U.S. South, see Culbert, David H. "World War II: the southern experience." in Kyvig (1976), pp. 112-128. For a summary of Florida, 1935-1946, see Gannon, Michael. 1993. *Florida, a short history*. Gainesville, FL: University Press of Florida, pp. 92-109.

190   199 "Austin Cary" A summary of the life of this great friend of the Forestry School of the University of Florida is given in Newins (1949).

190   200 "housing was swamped" The shortage of housing and office construction in one city is typical of the nation's experience in World War II, see Brinkley (1988).

191   201"increase in live births" *Historical Statistics of the United States, colonial times to 1970*. 1975. Washington, DC: U.S. Government Printing Office: 003-024-00120-9, Part 1, p. 49.

191   202 "Women ... were fired by the millions" Weatherford (1990), pp. 110-115, 128-198, 306-321.

191   203 "the G.I. Bill" Olson, Keith W. 1974. *The G.I. Bill, the Veterans, and the Colleges*. Lexington, KY: The University of Kentucky. Ross, Davis R. B. 1969. *Preparing for Ulysses, politics and veterans during World War II*. New York: Columbia University Press.

Merlin Dixon

192   204"my friend and forestry colleague" *Slash Pine Cache 1949*.

BIBLIOGRAPHY

Acheson, Dean. 1969. <u>Present at the Creation, My Years in the State Department</u>. New York: W. W. Norton & Company, Inc.

Akerman, Joe A., Jr. 1976. <u>Florida Cowman, a history of Florida cattle raising</u>. Kissimmee, FL: Florida Cattlemen's Association.

Asbell, Bernard. 1969. <u>When FDR Died</u>. New York: Holt, Rinehart and Winston.

Bell, Harold G. 1961. <u>Glimpses of the Panhandle</u>. Chicago: Adams Press.

Bishop, Jim. 1974. <u>FDR's Last Year, April 1944-April 1945</u>. New York: William Morrow.

Blount, Robert S. III. 1993. <u>Spirits of Turpentine, a history of Florida naval stores 1528-1950</u>. Florida Heritage Journal Monograph No. 3. Tallahassee, FL: Florida Agricultural Museum.

Bradford, Cdr. John W. Jr., USN (Ret.) 1994. "In pursuit of gold wings." <u>Foundation</u>, vol. 15, no. 2, pp. 56-64.

Brinkley, David. 1988. <u>Washington Goes to War</u>. New York: Ballentine Books.

Buell, Harold L. 1990. <u>Dauntless Helldivers, a dive-bomber pilot's epic story of the carrier battles</u>. New York: Orion Books.

Cabeza de Vaca. <u>The Journey of Alvar Nunez Cabeza de Vaca and his companions from Florida to the Pacific, 1528-1536</u>. Fanny Bandelier (Trans.) New York: A. S. Barnes & Company (1905); Allerton Book Co. (1922); AMS Press (1973).

Butow, Robert Joseph Charles. 1954. <u>Japan's Decision to Surrender</u>. Stanford, CA: Stanford University Press.

Chandler, David Leon. 1986. <u>Henry Flagler, the astonishing life and times of the visionary robber baron who founded Florida</u>. New York: Macmillan.

Colton, F. Barrows. 1940. "Aviation in commerce and defense." The National Geographic Magazine. vol. 78, no. 6, pp. 685-726.

Conrad, David Eugene. 1965. The Forgotten Farmers, the story of sharecroppers in the New Deal. Urbana, IL: University of Illinois Press.

Churchill, Jan. 1992. On Wings of War, Teresa James aviator. Manhattan, KS: Sunflower University Press.

Davis, Kenneth S. 1979. FDR, the New Deal years 1933-1937. New York: Random House.

Davis, Kenneth S. 1985. FDR, the New York years 1928-1933. New York: Random House.

Davis, Samuel A. Aviator's Flight Log Book #1. October 10, 1942 through May 31, 1946.

Davis, Samuel A. Aviator's Flight Log Book #2. June 1, 1945 through December 17, 1954.

Disinherited Speak, The: the story of sharecroppers in the New Deal. 1937. New York: The Workers Defense League for the Southern Tenant Farmers' Union.

Doyle, Don H. 1985. Nashville in the New South 1880-1930. Knoxville, TN: University of Tennessee Press, pp. 197, 215-216.

Edoin, Hoito. 1987. The Night Tokyo Burned. New York: St. Martin's Press.

Fire Fighter's Guide, Training Manual. 1983. Tallahassee, FL: Florida Department of Agriculture and Consumer Affairs.

Follett, Ken. 1991. Night Over Water. New York: William Morrow and Company.

Freidel, Frank. 1973. Franklin D. Roosevelt. Vols. 1-4. Boston: Little, Brown and Company.

Fuller, Walter P. 1954. <u>This Was Florida's Boom</u>. St. Petersburg, FL: Times Publishing Co.

Fuller, Walter P. 1972. <u>St. Petersburg and Its People</u>. St. Petersburg, FL: Great Outdoors Publishing Co.

Fusfeld, Daniel R. 1956. <u>The Economic Thought of Franklin D. Roosevelt and the Origins of the New Deal</u>. New York: Columbia University Press.

Fussell, Paul. "Thank God for the atomic bomb." <u>Washington Post</u>, August 23, 1981.

Gannon, Michael. 1993. <u>Florida, A Short History</u>. Gainesville, FL: University Press of Florida.

Gay, George H. 1979. <u>Sole Survivor, The Battle of Midway and its effects on his life</u>. Jersey City, NJ: 3B Litho.

Gillette, Michael L. 1986. <u>Texas in Transition</u>. Austin, TX: Lyndon Baines Johnson Library, School of Public Affairs, and Foundation.

<u>Golden Anniversary Celebration, Gulf County, Florida</u>. June 6-14, 1975. Chattanooga, TN: Great American Publishing Company.

Grosenbaugh, Lewis R. 1983. <u>History of the Florida Society of American Foresters</u>. Gainesville, FL: The Florida Society of American Foresters, SAF 83-10.

Guerrant, Edward O. 1960. <u>Herbert Hoover: Franklin Roosevelt, comparisons and contrasts</u>. Cleveland, OH: H. Allen.

Gunston, Bill. 1994. <u>World Encyclopedia of Aircraft Manufacturers</u>. Annapolis, MD: Naval Institute Press.

Halsey, William F. and Bryan, Joseph. 1947. <u>Admiral Halsey's Story</u>. New York: Whittlesey House.

Hill, Adm. Harry W. "A perfect amphibious assault." In Mason, John T., Jr. (Ed.) 1986. <u>The Pacific War Remembered, an oral history</u>

collection. Annapolis, MD: Naval Institute Press.

Historical Statistics of the United States, colonial times to 1970. 1975. Washington, DC: U.S. Government Printing Office: 003-024-00120-9, Part 1.

Hoyt, Edwin P. 1986. Japan's War, the great Pacific conflict 1853-1952. New York: McGraw-Hill Book Company.

Hutchison, Ira Augustus. 1951-1954. Some Who Passed This Way. Privately published from stories written for a Panama City weekly paper between November 29, 1951 and July 8, 1954.

Hynes, Samuel. 1988. Flights of Passage. New York: Frederic C. Beil.

Ivins, Molly. Molly Ivins Can't Say That, Can She?. New York: Random House.

Jane's Fighting Aircraft of World War II. 1946-47, 1989, 1992, 1994. New York: Crescent Boooks.

Karig, Capt. Walter, USNR, Harris, Lt. Cdr. Russell L., USNR, and Mason, Lt. Cdr. Frank A., USN. 1949. Battle Report, Victory in the Pacific. New York: Rinehart and Company, Inc.

Karig, Cdr. Walter, USNR, and Kelley, Lt. Welbourn, USNR. 1944. Battle Report, Pearl Harbor to Coral Sea. New York: Rinehart & Company, Inc.

Kauffman, Rear Adm. Draper. "The UDTs come of age." In Mason, John T., Jr. (Ed.) 1986. The Pacific War Remembered, oral history collection. Annapolis, MD: Naval Institute Press.

Keegan, John. 1989. The Second World War. New York: Viking.

Kimble, Warren F. 1969. The Most Unsordid Act, lend-lease, 1939-1941. Baltimore, MD: Johns Hopkins Press.

Knott, Capt. Richard C. 1979. The American Flying Boat. Annapolis, MD: Naval Institute Press.

Knott, Richard. 1984. <u>Black Cat Raiders of WW II</u>. Zebra.

Larrabee, Eric. 1987. <u>Commander in Chief, Franklin Delano Roosevelt, his lieutenants, and their war</u>. New York: Harper & Row Publishers.

Lea, Tom. 1957. <u>The King Ranch</u>. Boston: Little, Brown.

Leuthner, Stuart, and Jensen, Oliver. 1992. <u>High Honor</u>. Washington, DC: Smithsonian Institution Press.

Litz, Leo M. 1946. <u>Report from the Pacific</u>. Indianapolis: <u>The Indianapolis News</u>.

Litz, Leo M. "Report from the Pacific." <u>The Indianapolis News</u>. Tuesday, August 7, 1945.

Manchester, William. 1978. <u>American Caesar</u>. New York: Dell Publishing Co.

Manchester, William. 1979. <u>Goodbye Darkness, a memoir of the Pacific War</u>. Boston: Little, Brown and Company.

<u>Mark III Slipstream, The</u>. 1943. Corpus Christi, TX: Aviation Cadet Regiment of the U.S. Naval Air Station.

Martin, Sidney Walter. 1949. <u>Florida's Flagler</u>. Athens, GA: University of Georgia Press.

Mason, John T., Jr. (Ed.) 1986. <u>The Pacific War Remembered, an oral history collection</u>. Annapolis, MD: Naval Institute Press.

McCombs, Don and Worth, Fred L. 1983. <u>World War II, 4,139 strange and fascinating facts</u>. New York: Wing Books.

McCullough, David. 1992. <u>Truman</u>. New York: Simon & Schuster.

Morison, Samuel Elliot. 1947-1962. <u>History of United States Naval Operations in World War II</u>, XV vols. Boston: Little Brown and Co.

"More details on Navy exploits of Lieut. Davis." <u>The News Herald</u>,

Panama City, FL: October 28, 1946, p. 8.

Moroney, Rita L. 1985. History of the U.S. Postal Service, 1775-1984. Washington, DC: U.S. Government Printing Office: 1990-257-497/ 20076.

Newins, H. S. "The life of Austin Carey" [sic]. 1949. Slash Pine Cache 1949. Gainesville, FL: Forestry Club of the University of Florida, pp. 21-22, 55-57.

Newton, Wesley Phillips, and Rea, Robert S. (Ed.) 1987. Wings of Gold, an account of naval aviation training in World War II. Tuscaloosa, AL: The University of Alabama Press.

Oliver, William F. 1948. "Recent developments in naval stores operation." Slash Pine Cache 1948. Gainesville, FL: Forestry Club of the University of Florida.

Olson, Keith W. 1974. The G.I. Bill, the Veterans, and the Colleges. Lexington, KY: The University of Kentucky.

Onoda, Hiroo. 1974. No Surrender, my thirty-year war. Charles S. Terry (Trans.) Tokyo: Kodansha International Ltd. (Harper & Row, distributors).

Owen, A. L. Riesch. 1983. Conservation Under FDR. New York: Praefer Publishers.

Parker, Idella, with Keating, Mary. 1992. Idella, Marjorie Kinnan Rawlings' "perfect maid." Gainesville, FL: University Press of Florida.

Parrish, Thomas D. 1989. Roosevelt and Marshall: partners in politics and war. New York: William Morrow and Company.

Perkins, Frances. 1946. The Roosevelt I Knew. New York: The Viking Press.

Personnel of VP/VPB-33 with Mueller, Lt. A. J. USNR (Ret.) 1992. Black Cats with Wings of Gold. Philadelphia: Smith-Edwards-Dunlap Co.

Pisano, Dominick A. 1994. To Fill the Skies with Pilots, the civilian training program, 1939-46. Urbana, IL: University of Illinois Press.

Potter, E. B. 1976. <u>Nimitz</u>. Annapolis, MD: U.S. Naval Institute.

Powers, Elmer G. "Day by day on the farm, 1937." In Kyvig, David E. (Ed.) 1976. <u>FDR's America</u>. St. Charles, MO: Forum Press.

Prange, Gordon W. 1981. <u>At Dawn We Slept, the untold story of Pearl Harbor</u>. New York: Penguin Books.

Pyle, Ernie. 1944. <u>Brave Men</u>. New York: Henry Holt and Company.

Pyle, Ernie. 1946. <u>Last Chapter</u>. New York: Henry Holt and Company.

Quinn, David C. 1989. "Never a dull moment." in Leuthner, Stuart, and Jensen, Oliver (Ed.s) <u>High Honor</u>. Washington, DC: Smithsonian Institution Press.

Ramage, Vice Adm. Lawson P. "Wolf packs on the prowl." In Mason, John T. Jr. (Ed.) 1986. <u>The Pacific War Remembered, an oral history collection</u>. Annapolis, MD: Naval Institute Press.

Ramer, Robert. "The whole world was on fire." In Leuthner, Stuart, and Jensen, Oliver. 1992. <u>High Honor</u>. Washington, DC: Smithsonian Institution Press.

Rawlings, Marjorie Kinnan. 1938. <u>The Yearling</u>. New York: Charles Scribner's Sons.

Rigell, Joseph S., and Rigell, Elizabeth W. 1992. <u>Fired Again and Again, Praise the Lord!</u> Baltimore, MD: The Afikomen Company.

Roosevelt, Franklin D. Russell D. Buhite and David W. Levy (Ed.s) 1992. <u>FDR's Fireside Chats</u>. Norman, OK: University of Oklahoma Press.

Ross, Davis R. B. 1969. <u>Preparing for Ulysses, politics and veterans during World war II</u>. New York: Columbia University Press.

<u>San Patricio County in 1976, a bicentennial perspective</u>. 1976. Sinton,

TX: Sinton Bicentennial Celebrations.

Schrader, Richard K. "Bridging the Atlantic." <u>American History Illustrated</u>, vol. 23, no. 4, May, 1989, pp. 34-47.

Scruggs, Carroll Proctor (compiler). 1973. <u>Georgia Historical Markers</u>. Helen, GA: Bay Tree Grove.

<u>Seminole 1941</u>. Yearbook of the University of Florida.

<u>Seminole 1942</u>. Yearbook of the University of Florida.

<u>Seminole 1949</u>. Yearbook of the University of Florida.

Sidey, Hugh. "D-Day, the home front." <u>Time</u>, June 13, 1994, pp. 48-49.

Silverthorne, Elizabeth. 1988. <u>Marjories Kinnan Rawlings, sojourner at Cross Creek</u>. Woodstock, NY: Overlook Press.

<u>Slash Pine Cache 1949</u>. Gainesville, FL: Forestry Club of the University of Florida.

Smith, Gene. 1970. <u>The Shattered Dream, Herbert Hoover and the great depression</u>. New York: Morrow.

Sowinski, Larry. 1981. <u>Action in the Pacific, as seen by U.S. Navy photographers during World War 2</u>. Annapolis, MD: Naval Institute Press.

Spector, Ronald H. 1985. <u>Eagle Against the Sun</u>. New York: The Free Press.

Stoler, Mark A. 1989. <u>George C. Marshall: a soldier-statesman of the American centruy</u>. Boston: Twayne Publishers.

Strahan, Jerry E. 1994. <u>Andrew Jackson Higgins and the Boats That Won World War II</u>. Baton Rouge, LA: Louisiana State Univesity Press.

Swanborough, Gordon, and Bowers, Peter M. 1968. <u>United States</u>

Aircraft Since 1911. New York: Funk & Wagnalls.

Terkel, Studs. 1984. *The Good War, an oral history of World War II*. New York: Pantheon Press.

Terkel, Studs. 1970. *Hard Times, an oral history of the great depression*. New York: Pantheon Books.

Texas, a Guide to the Lone Star State. 1940. New York: Hastings House.

TEXAS State Travel Guide. 1993. Texas Department of Transportation, Travel and Information Division, P. O. Box 5064, Austin, Texas, 78763-5064.

Thorne, Christopher. 1978. *Allies of a Kind, the United States, Britain and the war against Japan*. New York: Oxford Univesity Press.

Time-Life Books Editors. 1989. *WW II: Time-Life Books History of the Second World War*. New York: Prentice-Hall Press.

Truman, Harry S. 1955. *Memoirs by Harry S. Truman, Year of Decisions*. New York: Doubleday & Company, Inc.

Turnbull, Capt. Archibald D., and Lord, Lt. Cdr. Clifford L. 1949. *History of United States Naval Aviation*. New Haven, CT: Yale University Press.

Wallace, Lucille Forgy. *Forgy, Forgey, and Forgie Family History*. Privately published, in the collection of Lona Davis Spencer.

Weintraub, Stanley. 1991. *Long Day's Journey into War, December 7, 1941*. New York: Truman Talley Books, Dutton.

Weatherford, Dorothy. 1990. *American Women and World War II*. New York: Facts on File.

Weems, Lt. Cdr. P. V. H., USN (Ret.) 1938. *Air Navigation*. 2nd edition. New York: McGraw-Hill Book Co. Inc.

West, G. M. 1960 (4th edition). <u>St. Andrews Florida</u>. St. Andrew, FL: Panama City Publishing Company.

Womack, Marlene. 1994. <u>Along the Bay, a pictorial history of Bay County</u>. Norfolk, VA: Pictorial Heritage Publishing Co.

Wood, Virginia S. 1981. <u>Live Oaking: southern timber for tall ships</u>. Boston: Northwestern University.

Lona Davis Spencer was born nine months and three days after her father returned to her mother after World War II. In her Florida childhood, she took her elders' fishing, farming, and forestry lore for granted, unaware that their way of life would die with them.

She first heard the story of Sam's Navy Cross at the 25th reunion of crew 5 of the Willie 7. With her father's chronicle, the story of a young man's quest to go somewhere and be somebody takes shape. In this book she has the privilege of telling the world what a boy from the backwoods can do and be. She lives with her husband and son in Nashville, Tennessee, and writes a regular Op-Ed column for the *Nashville Banner.*